TRUE
SISTERS

Volume I

TRUE SISTERS

Volume 1

From the Editors
Of *True Story* And
True Confessions

Published by True Renditions, LLC

True Renditions, LLC
105 E. 34th Street, Suite 141
New York, NY 10016

Visit us on the web at www.truerenditionsllc.com.

Contents

SAND DOLLAR WISHES
Will they ever come true for me?

I sat alone at the window table, watching the tide roll in. I'd ventured back to the Sea Shack for the first time since Corinne married and moved three states away, and just sitting at "our regular table" made me feel closer to my twin sister.

Of course, our worlds have been close (to say the least) since the day we were born. But now we were divided by a celebration that should've made me feel ecstatically happy for her. Instead, I just felt . . . guilty. While one part of me wanted to rejoice for my sister's marvelous good fortune . . . a darker, meaner part of me wanted to hate the fact that she found her knight—

Leaving me in solitude for the first time in my whole life.

Alan tinkered behind the bar, wearing the trademark soft, green polo shirt required by all the staff at the Sea Shack. He retied a clean bar apron over ironed jeans that creased perfectly over sockless, tanned feet slid into deck shoes. He took the meal orders of those who chose to sit in the immediate bar area instead of the main floor. He'd served Corinne and me for two years, often kidding us with smiley faces on the bill and threats to abduct both of us and carry us off to his beach house. Needless to say, he had us drooling before we ever thought about lunch.

"Better watch what you ask for, Alan," we'd tease. "You might not know how to handle both of us," one or the other of us would reply. Our natural camaraderie flowed easy and we fed each other's thoughts. I liked to think that Alan favored me, but one could never tell—especially with Corinne around.

Corinne played more. She was the flirt, which is probably why she got married first. I used her throughout high school and most of college to break the ground with guys. Boys gravitated toward her.

Granted we look so much alike, but Corinne has the hint of flare. We could dress alike, yet she'd don the sparkly earrings while I wore the hoops. She'd use twice the eye shadow and line her lips, but I'd stick with basic mascara and lip-gloss. I'd wear a watch and she'd flaunt six bracelets. She was exciting to be around, and she invigorated me.

On the other hand, I toned Corinne down. At the bars, I restricted her to three margaritas or four beers. When her jokes danced on the line of risqué, I changed the subject. A loser hit on her one evening when she'd reached her limit on tequila, and I lured him off and sent him on his way. Yep, Corinne and I were the perfect compliment. Together, we composed the consummate girl. Apart, I saw us as half-empty glasses of water. Then she found her other half in Cody.

The wedding was two months ago. Sitting there at our table overlooking the water, I almost wished I that I didn't go back to the Sea Shack. The memories acted as a quasi-connection to Corinne, but without her physically seated across the table I felt alone. That time I faced socializing with Alan without Corinne's sense of humor and fluttering eyelashes. Exposed and plain, I'd even forgotten to wear earrings.

"Long time no see," Alan said as he flipped over the paper to take my new order.

"Shrimp salad sandwich with no mayo, sparkling water, and key lime pie," I said. Corinne's usual order. Alan recognized it, too, from the raised eyebrow.

"I take it Corinne is coming. The usual for you, too?" he asked. I always ate a Caesar salad garnished with crabmeat, iced tea, and no dessert. I'd steal a bite of Corinne's pie and then brag about not being a slave to sweets.

"Corinne's not here, Alan. She and Cody are still busy being newlyweds seven hundred miles away."

Eww. That doesn't sound nice at all. Alan tapped his pen on the top of his pad and waited for me to decide whom I am and what I wanted to eat. He smiled in spite of the confusion, probably thinking that I ordered for Corinne from sheer habit.

"I'll eat Corinne's usual today. I know it sounds weird, but I crave shrimp. And I can't sneak a bite of pie if it's not sitting on the table."

He looked at me with a hint of pity. I don't need that. Well, maybe I do. I'm pitying myself, so why can't he?

"I'll put the order in. Be back in a sec with your water," Alan said with a wink.

He never approached us to ask either of us out. That's the problem with being a twin in the presence of the other twin—a boy can't approach one girl without wondering what the other girl thought. After all, what would initially attract a boy to one of us and not the other?

Alan knows both of us, if you consider waitering for two straight years a social connection. He has the opposite problem of most guys. He knows us well enough to tell us apart, so how was he to ask one of us out and not worry about insulting the other since he'd flirted with both of us for so long? I figured he has someone on the side that prevents him from entertaining one or the other of us.

Paranoia ruled my day. I wondered what to do, what to say,

and expecting someone to finish my sentences. I can't decide what sweater to buy without Corinne's advice, or how to change my hair without her artful hand. Just sitting here makes me. . . .

"You miss Corinne?" Alan asked, setting my water on a soft, green napkin.

I reached for the water just for something to do. "Yes, I do. A lot."

"I haven't seen either of you since the wedding. How did it go? I feel like I was practically there after listening to all of the plans for six months. You wore lavender, tea-length dresses, right? Or did you change to the powder blue?" He pretended to prance like a little girl, dropping a napkin for an invisible gentleman to pick up. He bent over and picked it up, giving me a waft of his body wash.

Two middle-aged ladies seated near the wall smiled at Alan. I giggled.

"We went with the blue. She almost changed to long, black dresses," I said to the top of his head before he stood up.

"Black? That might've been classy. I could see her doing that," he said, straightening up.

"Only Corinne."

"Yep, only Corinne. Gotta get back to work. Your shrimp salad ought to be up in a jiffy."

"Thanks, Alan."

I turned to daydream out the window. The luxury of air conditioning let me bask cozy in the sun's rays. I watched the beachcombers wander up the beach, some headed to the Sea Shack. As a native, I knew the times to wander the sand and avoid so many people, see the most creatures, and find the best shells. Corinne knew, too.

In high school, we knew every grain of sand and every bronzed boy in the surf. We played off each other, often changing bikinis in the middle of the day just to throw off the guys ogling us. At night we laid awake scheming how to confuse yet another newcomer, and decided who would date which one first. We became "those beach twins" to the entire town's population.

College took us to separate cities, but the summers always brought us back together at the beach. Our cavorting evolved from frolicking to lengthy strolls and deep mature conversation along the foamy water. Once we graduated, Corinne on May fifth and me on May sixth, we returned home. Corinne taught ninth grade, her silliness enthralling the young teens. Of course I studied education, too, but I preferred the spongy, open minds of second graders.

The best time to dodge the worst crowds in the summer is noon on Tuesdays; that day became our biweekly rendezvous at Sea Shack.

"Excuse me, honey."

I jerked around to see an elderly woman, one of the patrons seated against the wall earlier.

"Yes?"

"Just wanted to say that you better grab that young man before someone else does. He's sweet enough to eat, and he's definitely fond of you." She nodded up and down with each word, like a bobble head doll.

I smiled respectfully. "Thanks. He is cute, isn't he?"

"Amen, honey. He got my blood moving, that's for sure." She laughed. I laughed as well at the vision of a gray-haired woman mauling Alan. She waved good-bye and met her friend at the entrance. They whispered together and the second woman put one hand over her mouth and pushed her friend on the shoulder with the other. They'd probably giggle over Alan all afternoon.

"What was that about?" he asked as he stepped up to place my meal on the table.

"They think you're cute," I said, unwilling to relay the rest of the chat.

He rolled his eyes. "Just what I need, a centerfold offer for AARP Magazine. Wait, how much do you think they'd pay me? Hey, I could dye my hair gray!"

"You're full of yourself today, aren't you?"

"Something in the water, I guess. Flag me if you need something else. The lunch crowd is getting deadly!"

I put a shrimp in my mouth and wished that I'd ordered my crabmeat Caesar salad. My fork moved the pink shrimp around on my plate before I speared another one. As I chewed, I looked back out the window, craving the sand under my feet. Maybe I'll take a walk after lunch is over.

Corinne and I always took our beach walks before our lunch dates and we collected sand dollars. The North Carolina beach is known for them. I have a collection of our best specimens framed in my living room at home, accented with pastel mats and a brass frame. I fingered the tiny one on my necklace that Corinne gave me as a bridesmaid gift.

The best place to collect sand dollars is around Limey Pier. Corinne declared each search a contest. The sand dollar had to be the smallest, the largest, the whitest, or the fattest to make the search more entertaining.

We carefully tucked each chalky skeleton in an old peach basket lined with a beach towel decorated with seahorses, left over from our childhood days. I carried the basket toward the pier and she carried it back. At the bottom of the steps leading up to Sea Shack's umbrella deck, we dusted our feet, slipped back into sandals or sneakers, and stepped inside to order lunch.

4

Inside the restaurant, we marveled over the intricacies of the pieces we found. Alan often served as the impartial judge in determining which sister found the best treasure of the day. The winner received a lemonade with a paper umbrella spearing a cherry.

"Beautiful beach day," he said, looking outside over the top of my head. I didn't hear him come over.

"Yeah, it really is. Glad I came out today. I've missed this place."

He hesitated like he was choosing his words. ESP told me that he wanted to say that he missed my presence. When he didn't, my cheeks turned pink, embarrassed at my willingness to listen to an old lady with hot flashes.

"I think the place missed you, too. You girls were practically fixtures here. The beach twins."

The familiar nickname sounded good. I lied when I said, "I forgot all about our title, Alan. How'd you remember it? Horny, acne-faced little boys called us that about ten years ago," I said with a smile.

"Can't remember where I heard that, but it fits. How's the shrimp?"

"Not as good as the crabmeat salad. I think I have better taste in food than Corinne, except for the key lime pie. I wish I had half her sparkle and daring. Calories never bothered her. She so lives for the moment."

Alan grinned. "I thought you have half of whatever she has. Isn't that how twins are supposed to work?"

"Not always. She had me beat hands down in a lot of ways—including finding a guy. She could attract a man from three miles away with only her smile and a giggle." Including Alan, I thought.

"She's a special girl. You done with your dishes? I'll leave your pie here in case you want to pick at it some more."

"That's fine."

I bet that the wedding plans scared him away. A girl talking about marriage is like garlic to a vampire, and he listened to a double dose for months. I envisioned him relaxing at the reception with a piece of wedding cake, our shoes kicked off under a canopied table from dancing too long.

I'm rebounding, I thought. Not from the loss of a guy, but from the loss of a sister. This is stupid. I snatched another bite of the pie and pulled the napkin out of my lap and set it on the table. I waved at Alan.

I reached for my purse. "Could you bring me the check, Alan? I'm stepping into the ladies' room for a second." I slid out of the rattan chair and walked around the atrium planter of philodendron to the restroom.

I shook my head at my reflection and my lunacy. I vowed to leave the Sea Shack and head to the community college and sign up

5

for a couple of classes. That would occupy my mind until I could set it back to right and return to my kids in September. Hands washed and lipstick adjusted, I exited the restroom toward the table. The tablecloth was cleared completely of dishes, condiments, and silverware. Even from a distance I noted how neat the table had been cleaned in the short time I was gone. Alan always did a great job. As I got closer, however, I noted one item still in the middle of the table.

A soft, green napkin displayed a lone, white sand dollar. A circle of sand had been drizzled around it, the sun causing it to glitter. The dollar was one of the largest and most perfect I ever saw.

My breath caught in my throat. I looked around, but no one watched me. I lowered myself in the chair and reached for the shell. Lifting it, I found these words on the napkin: My turn to walk you to Limey Pier. Alone at last—Alan.

THE END

BEATEN BY THE
MAN SHE LOVED
Now her kids will pay the price

I brushed my sister's hair from her forehead and smiled into her vacant face. As usual, there was no recognition in her eyes. She stared past me without blinking, seemingly focused on nothing.

The elderly lady in the next bed snored loudly. Down the hall I heard a man begging to be let out of his wheelchair. "I want to go home," he cried, over and over.

I couldn't blame him, in spite of his dementia. The nursing home was clean, and the staff worked hard, but the rooms still smelled like stale lunch and dried urine. The few visitors seemed to leave after only a few minutes of visiting their relatives.

Oh, Marsha, I thought to myself. Why did it have to come to this? I held her limp hand in mine. As her mouth hung partly open, saliva slipped down her chin. I wiped it away with a tissue, my eyes filled with tears.

Marsha had always been the beautiful girl and I'd been the tomboy. She had three guys ask her to the senior prom. Me? I had none. She planned to become a teacher. I had no idea what I wanted to do until I graduated from high school.

As I looked at my sister, strapped into a chair in her room at the nursing home, I could only think of how ironic it all was. My parents, our relatives and friends, they all thought Marsha would succeed and do well. It was her little sister, tomboy Maria that people whispered about.

I did study and earn good grades, but it was my sister the boys wanted to date. When the phone rang in the evenings it was always for her. She was elected president of her high school class, was homecoming queen her junior year, and in a bathing suit I thought she could easily make the cover of one of those men's sports magazines.

I had a group of friends, but we were all more interested in sports than boys. I used to say, "What would some guy see in me?" My idea of the perfect girl to date was my sister, and lots of guys thought so, too. Besides, the guys in my class seemed so immature and I just never did get the hang of flirting, anyway. Time for all that stuff later, I'd tell myself.

I remembered the time my aunt told Mom, "You'd better watch Maria. She'll never amount to half of what Marsha will."

That really hurt, but I never let them know I overheard the

conversation. By this time I wondered if there was something wrong with me and, being honest with myself, at times I was jealous of Marsha.

Unfortunately, I'd proved them all wrong. Now I was a teacher and doing well. My sister was in a half-conscious state, and had been for six months, ever since Al beat her up the final time.

I gritted my teeth when I thought of Al. Handsome, proud, cocky, the life of the party, built like a star football player, tall, you name it. Al had it all. Except decency.

I thought about the first time he came to our house to pick Marsha up for a date. She'd just started college and met Al at a friend's party the week before. Marsha could've had her pick of guys, and Al knew it. I figured he decided he had to have her to prove he could.

They started to date steadily. I truly wanted Marsha to dump the guy. When I tried to talk to her about Al one night, after they'd been dating for a few months, she just stared at me.

"You're jealous, aren't you, Maria?" Marsha said, hands on her hips, head tilted back. "Al is the most popular guy I know." She checked her lipstick in the mirror. "His dad owns the top car dealership in town. Al will go right to work for his dad once he graduates. His future is set." She looked directly at me. "So don't you worry about Al and me, little sister, 'cause we'll do just fine."

I slowly shook my head. "Maybe I've been jealous of you in the past, but not this time. I don't like the guy, Marsha. I don't trust him."

She laughed. "As if you're some big judge of men." Flipping her hair back, she grinned at me, then walked out to meet Al.

Well, she was right on one score. I hadn't dated all that much. Sure, once in a while I'd been jealous of Marsha, but not this time. This time I was worried.

Her words stung, though, and I never mentioned it again. Now I wish I had.

At least I wasn't alone in my thoughts. I heard my folks quietly talking about Al a couple of times. I know Mom was especially concerned.

Marsha had dated Al six months when she announced she was pregnant and quitting college. "I'll go back someday," she said.

My poor folks were so upset, but they put on a smile and gave Marsha a nice wedding and reception. I was the maid of honor in a wedding I hoped would never be.

I watched Marsha at the reception, all smiles and glowing. I watched Al, too. When Marsha wasn't watching I saw him grope inside one of the bridesmaid's dresses. He turned and saw me watching him, a sneaky smile on his face.

I felt sick inside, and let myself out a side door and stood on the patio. My head lowered, I didn't hear someone follow me.

"You okay?" a masculine voice asked.

I whirled around and nearly bumped into a tall guy. My face must've shown my shock and fear.

"Don't worry, please," he said. "I just noticed you leave the reception and you looked a little pale." He hesitated a minute, then put out his hand. "I'm Marc Rizzo. Sure didn't mean to scare you."

"If you were at the wedding, I guess you know I'm Maria, Marsha's sister," I said. "You're a friend of Al?"

A brief frown flashed across his face before he answered. "No, actually my sister and Al's cousin went to school together, and I was sort of recruited as an escort, mainly I think because I have a car big enough for a group of young women."

Tall, not pretty-boy handsome, but good-looking in a rugged way, square jaw, and with beautiful eyes, Marc seemed troubled by something.

"Has your sister known Al long?" he asked.

"Six months. Why do you ask?"

He hesitated a few seconds, then managed a little smile. "No reason, nothing important."

I knew that whatever it was, it was important. I wondered if he'd tell me someday. I wondered if I'd see him again. To my surprise, I wanted to.

Music drifted in from the reception hall. As the wind from the open doorway softly pushed the curtains in the room aside, I saw Marsha and Al dancing. My heart lurched. I saw only trouble for my sister.

I looked up at Marc and noticed him watching me. "Do you like to dance?" he asked.

I bit my lip. "I don't know, to be honest. I haven't been to many dances."

"Really?" he asked. "A beautiful young woman like you?"

I laughed. "My sister is the beautiful one."

He shook his head. "You haven't looked in the mirror lately, Maria." He took my hand. "Let's see how we do."

We did great, mainly because Marc was such a good dancer, a great leader. It would've been hard not to be able to dance with a guy like him. I loved being in his arms and feeling the beat of the music. I enjoyed myself more than I could ever remember.

Marc drove me home that night. He stopped the engine after he drove into our driveway, and then turned to look at me. "Maria, I can't remember when I've enjoyed an evening more. I hate to say this, but tomorrow I leave to work on a big contracting project in New York. I'll be gone over six months."

9

I looked down at my hands. Darn it all, anyway. Here I was a senior in high school, finally met the best guy—who even seemed to like me—and he was leaving.

"I'll be back someday," Marc said. He lightly traced his finger across my cheek. "I hope we can get together again. And I hope the fact I'm five years older doesn't scare you."

"You don't scare me at all," I whispered.

He leaned over and lightly brushed his lips across mine. I'd been kissed before, but never like that. I wondered if he felt the electricity that I did. It seemed like all the little hairs on my arms stood to attention saying, "More, more!" The moment was over much too soon.

Marc walked me to the door, said good-bye, and was gone. I didn't hear from him again. For a while my heart was crushed, but I knew he'd probably found a real woman, someone more his age, someone who'd been around, as they say.

Like Marsha, I decided I wanted to be a teacher, too. With my good grades I was given several small scholarships. That money, along with my part-time job, helped me get through college. My folks didn't have the money and I didn't ask them.

My sister had told me not to talk to her anymore about Al, so I didn't. I was busy with my class studies, carrying a full load, plus my part-time job. Occasionally I dated some guys, and went steady with one I met at work, but eventually I broke that off. He was okay, but in the back of my mind I guess I compared everyone with Marc, and no one measured up.

I moved into an apartment with three other students and was rarely at home. We lived by the university, and all four of us struggled with classes, jobs, and a constant lack of money. We got along well, though, and each month managed to scrape up enough for the rent and utilities. If one of us was short one month, we made it up, knowing we'd probably have a short month ourselves. Three of us were waitresses and depended a lot on tips, and those sure could vary from one week to the next. At least we got meals free when we worked.

I was invited to a friend's wedding. I thought about Marc that night as I sat in the church pew, and wondered where he was, thinking he'd probably gotten married by now. I was sure he'd probably forgotten me, just a kid in his eyes, the night his lips had softly brushed mine. My pulse still picked up when I remembered that kiss.

As I watched the bride walk down the aisle, I wondered about Marsha. I hadn't heard anything, other than she was pregnant. In a way that bothered me, not hearing anything. I assumed Mom knew I was busy enough without hearing about my sister. I made a mental note to call Marsha the next week.

I never made that call. A message waited for me when I got home, to call Mom and Dad right away. There wasn't any answer, so all I could do was wait. I tried to study, but my mind kept returning to the urgent message. I finally fell asleep on the couch. The phone woke me after midnight.

"Maria, it's Mom." She hesitated for a few seconds, and I thought I heard her crying quietly. "Marsha's been hurt, Maria. Can you come to the hospital and be with your dad and me?"

I didn't ask any questions. I just went. Sitting in the emergency room reception area when I arrived, my folks suddenly looked much older, as if they'd aged ten years in the last one.

I put my hands on their shoulders. They stood, wrapped their arms around me, and cried.

"Excuse me," someone said. A young woman stood next to us. "I'm Dr. Carnes. I'm sorry to bother you, but I'd like to talk to you about Marsha."

I was still in a fog about what had happened, but I'd definitely picked up on the fact that Al wasn't around. Dr. Carnes looked at the chart in her hands. "Marsha has a fractured jaw and a badly bruised cheek and eye. She has other bruises and contusions that will heal over time. She'll be moved to the ward within an hour. She'll probably be here a few days and then she can go home. There will need to be follow-up visits of course, especially for her jaw."

My folks just nodded, as if in a stupor. Before I could ask what happened, a policeman walked up. Tall, middle-aged, a kindly look on his face, he asked us to sit down.

"Al Helder should be in jail," the policeman said. "However, Marsha refuses to implicate him. She denies he hit her, and says she fell down a flight of stairs. Unless we have something to go on, we can't hold him."

"You can't just let him go," I said, as I clutched his arm, my worst fears having come true. I was right about Al after all, but that didn't make me feel good about it.

"Lady, your sister insists she was in an accident and there are no witnesses."

Marsha'd never told me Al mistreated her, but I'd always wondered. Al was too selfish, too jealous, too cocky and full of himself, to make a good husband. He was the kind of man the psychologists warn girls to stay away from. There was one important person in the world to Al, and that was Al.

There was nothing any of us could do. Marsha refused to admit to my folks that Al had mistreated her. She spent only a day in the hospital, and then Al picked her up and took her home. Two weeks later, Eva was born.

That was the beginning of many trips to the ER for Marsha. Even after Eva was born, and then Brendan a year later, Marsha continued to defend Al. The police, emergency room staff, my folks, and me—we all tried to get her to tell the truth. Trouble was, she insisted she was telling the truth.

When I confronted her one evening in the ER, she yelled at me that I was just jealous, and that if she were a better wife Al would be a good husband. I stared at my sister, and suddenly saw her in a different light.

She'd always been so beautiful and self-confident that I'd kept that image in my mind. Now I realized how thin she'd become, she had no makeup on, and there was a frightened look in her eyes. I also saw defiance, and nothing I could say would change her mind, because she still saw me as the jealous, younger sister.

For the next several years I saw little of Marsha. Eva and Brendan were often at my folks' house. In fact I sometimes wondered if they spent more time there than with Marsha and Al. That was probably for the best, though—at least they were out of harm's way.

Marsha landed in ER one too many times, and several years after that first incidence, Al was finally arrested. The DA's office finally felt they had enough to go on, I guess, but Al was out on bail within hours. His father hired a good lawyer, and since Al's family had plenty of money, bail was quickly posted.

If nothing else, Al was a good car salesman, and soon he was running the dealership while his folks traveled. Money was never a problem. His folks treated Marsha like the daughter they'd never had, and probably just couldn't believe their son would beat up his wife.

When Eva was three and Brendan two, things seemed to settle down for Marsha and Al, at least from what I gathered. Mom told me one day that she thought Al had finally "grown up." I hoped so, but I had my doubts. Still, almost six months went by without any problems, or at least I never heard of any. We'd never been close. I hoped that would change.

Now, as I sat in the nursing home, my hand on Marsha's arm, I knew we never would become close. Marsha's brain would never heal. She'd never be Marsha again.

In a fit of anger Al had beaten Marsha so severely one night, when dinner was late and Brendan was crying, that my sister was permanently damaged beyond repair. Now she was in a nursing home and he was in jail, waiting trial.

An aide came in to change Marsha and get her ready for dinner, and I left for home. I walked out into the fresh air, leaving the nursing home smells of bleach and disinfectant and other odors behind, and took a deep breath of the fresh air outside. A soft rain tapped on my shoulders as I quickly walked to the car.

Just as I reached for my car door, a man behind me asked, "Don't I know you?" I jerked around, my hand on the car door in case I needed to jump in quickly.

He walked up to me. He was right. We had met before. Marc. Almost five years had passed, but I'd recognize him anywhere.

He stood before me. "Maria Keats. Seems like whenever we meet I'm startling you." He smiled. "You're looking good. How are you?"

Better, now that I've seen you again, I wanted to say. I hesitated. I wasn't all that good, to tell the truth. The last six months hadn't been good at all.

"I'm sorry," Marc said. "Seems like I caught you at a bad time." He tilted his head toward the nursing home. "Do you have a parent or grandparent here?"

I slowly shook my head. "My sister," I whispered.

"Oh, no," he said. "Look, can we get out of the rain? There's a restaurant next door. Maybe you'll let me buy you dinner."

I don't think I really answered. He gently took my hand and we walked to the restaurant. I noticed his left hand, holding mine, had no ring. I wondered if he had a girlfriend. Certainly someone as wonderful as Marc wasn't still available.

We ordered the lasagna special, and after a few minutes of small talk, told each other about our lives since we'd met that one time, at Marsha's wedding.

"The nursing home is looking for a contractor to remodel an older unit, so my dad and I are putting in a bid on it," Marc said. "I've thought about you since that night, Maria. I almost called you, more than once, but you were in high school, and I'm five years older. Just didn't seem right at the time."

I almost told him that age no longer mattered, now that I was a grown woman, and a professional one at that. I couldn't tell him I'd compared every other man I met to him, after seeing him only once. So instead I talked about Marsha, and why I was at the nursing home.

Marc laid his hand on mine. "I never did trust Al," he said. "I'd heard about him from my kid sister, and what I heard wasn't all that good."

I took a deep breath. "I didn't like him either, but Marsha got upset when I tried to warn her about him. She thought I was jealous. I don't deny I might've been before, because she was so popular, but I sure wasn't jealous of her being with Al. I just wanted the guy gone, out of the picture. I think my folks felt the same."

Marc lightly squeezed my hand. "You don't realize what a prize you are, young lady." He lightly touched my cheek, the way he'd done years before, and I remembered how I'd felt then. It was no different now. I told myself a girl couldn't fall in love in a few minutes. Then I remembered that's exactly what my mother had done.

Marc was frequently at the nursing home because they did get the remodeling contract. I was there almost every day, visiting Marsha. He'd stop in to say hello for a minute and talk a bit. After a week, he asked me to go out with him.

Marc and I began to date steadily and for the first time in a very long while, there was happiness in my life. I loved him; I knew that for sure now, although what he saw in me I couldn't imagine.

Every minute spent with Marc was precious. They talk about soul mates. I used to think that was just something a person said. Now I knew it was true. Much of our time was spent cooking dinner together or taking simple walks in the evenings or bringing Marsha's children to my place where all four of us watched a video.

Our time together was more limited than he wanted, not because of the children, who he adored, but because I was busy taking care of Marsha, and coordinating with the DA's office. My goal in life was to see Al go to prison for as long as possible, and that one goal just about ruled my life. I couldn't let go of my hatred for Al.

When Al's parents begged me to realize he was very sorry for what he'd done and he should be allowed to return to society and not go to jail, I about lost it. I figured that if I didn't fight for my sister, no one would. Their attorney was well-known in high profile defense cases. What chance did I have against someone like him? It didn't matter. I had to try, because if I didn't, no one would. I was on the phone to the prosecutor's office three or four times a week, following up on what they were doing.

After several months of dating, Marc asked me to marry him. I looked at this big man and traced my finger around his lips. I leaned my head against his chest and listened to his heartbeat. He was so important to me. I felt so lucky to be with him.

I wanted to marry him. I loved him. But I had to take care of Marsha first, and make sure Al went to prison for as long as the law allowed. Nothing was more important to me.

"Give me six months, Marc." I looked up into his eyes. "That's not so long, is it? By then Al should be in prison, hopefully for a very long time."

"And maybe he won't be, Maria. Maybe he'll be set free, or on probation, or given a short sentence. What then?"

"That just can't be," I said.

We left it at that, although uneasiness settled over me. I felt him pull away, emotionally if not physically. Surely he could see how important this fight was, couldn't he?

My folks weren't doing well. Dad had the beginnings of dementia, and Mom's heart was failing. They'd taken care of the two children, now four and three, but it was obvious that couldn't continue.

I stopped over one night and talked to Mom. "I'll take the kids," I said. "You can't raise them, and Al's family shouldn't have them. They belong with us."

Mom's eyes filled with tears as she held a tissue to her eyes. She put her hand on my arm. "You always were the girl I could rely on," she said through her tears. "Everyone thought Marsha would do so well, but I knew your day would come. You've become such a beautiful woman, too, Maria." She wrapped her arms around me and hung on tightly.

I brought Eva and Brendan home with me. The next day I contacted an attorney to start legal proceedings, to give me permanent custody. Working full-time, picking up the children at day-care, conferring with the district attorney about the looming trial, and visiting Marsha every day, my days were so filled I usually collapsed into bed around midnight, exhausted.

Marc came over once or twice a week and helped me fix dinner for the kids. They adored him.

As I watched him read to them one evening, I said, "You'll make a wonderful father, Marc."

Later he said, "I'd like to be their father, Maria. And I can be if we get married."

"Oh, Marc, I love you so much." I leaned against his big chest. I felt so protected with him.

But I had all these obligations to take care of first. "Soon, Marc," I said. "Soon."

"You can't solve Marsha's problems, Maria," he said. "She made her choices, and I hate to say it, but everyone saw it coming and she wouldn't believe anyone." He tilted my chin up. "Look at me, Maria. Nothing's going to change. Marsha will never be better. You can't change that. And the DA doesn't need your help in taking care of Al."

"I can't abandon her," I said.

He slowly shook his head. "Of course not, and I didn't say that. But you don't need to visit her every day, not with all your other obligations. I'm willing to help in any way I can. I want to be the father of these kids, but only if you'll start to think of something other than Marsha and getting back at Al."

"The trial starts soon," I said. "It's been put off so many times by that pricey lawyer that Al's father hired, and finally it's going to court. I've got to be there."

"Why, Maria? Why?"

15

I shrugged and held up my hands. "Marc, Marsha needs me."

"In what way?" he asked. "What can you do for her now? Don't you think the children need you more? Don't you think I need you more?"

As I lay in bed alone that night, exhausted from another day of working, picking up the children, visiting Marsha after dinner, and arguing with Marc, my mind was like a kaleidoscope, whirling with thoughts. None of my so-called solutions seemed workable, unless I abandoned Marsha.

Mom wasn't well, Dad was probably going into a nursing home for dementia patients, and neither could visit Marsha any longer.

After talking to the DA one day on my lunch break, I almost cried. Now he was telling me that Al was going to plead temporary insanity. That would mean Al could possibly go to the state mental hospital, and even be released in a few years!

Everything seemed to go from bad to worse. I felt as if I was in the vortex of a whirlpool, being pulled down into the depths, reaching up my hands for help that never came.

Even the DA told me I should "relax" and let him handle it. "We're going after this guy, Maria. There's nothing more you can do right now."

But that evening when I visited Marsha, her nightgown had food stains on it, and it was obvious she hadn't been bathed that day. I washed her face and arms, found a clean nightgown, and somehow managed to change her clothes by myself. Again, it was almost midnight by the time I got home. I paid the baby-sitter, collapsed in bed, and was up again before six to feed Brendan and Eva and get them off to day-care.

The next week another hearing for Al was scheduled. Mom called and suggested I skip it. "There's nothing you can do, Maria. Let the DA's office handle it and get on with your own life with your nice young man."

Nice young man? Suddenly I realized I hadn't heard from Marc for almost a week. I put my head in my hand and leaned my elbow on the table. I sat there for what seemed like a long time.

Slowly, I dialed Marc's number. No answer. I left a message. "Marc, I've missed you. Please call."

The weekend went by with no message from Marc. I took the kids to the zoo and the library, trying to make up for time lost that they both needed so much. Poor kids. Their mother in a semi-vegetative state in a nursing home, their father in jail. They depended on me, too.

By Monday morning I was worried about Marc and hoped I'd see him at the nursing home, where the construction was in progress. I called my principal and asked for the day off, then took the children

16

to visit their mother that morning. They hadn't seen her in months, and I didn't want them to forget her.

As usual, she didn't respond to either child, and both kids seemed anxious to leave. As I watched the scene, I finally realized that life would always be this way for Marsha. I would never abandon her, but her children needed me more than their mother did. Marc told me he needed me, and that brought a warm glow to my heart, because I needed him, too.

I also couldn't change what would happen to Al in court. That was up to the district attorney's office and the court system. I would testify if asked, but other than that, I had to admit I wasn't much help in the case.

I took the children's hands and said, "Time to go, kids." We walked out to the construction site.

I saw Marc right away, several inches taller than most of the men, his suntanned arms holding blueprints, talking to one of the foremen. How did he feel about me? Why hadn't I heard from him?

I didn't know what to do and felt I shouldn't interfere. He hadn't returned my calls. My love for him overwhelmed me, and yet I just stood there.

My decision was solved by Brendan, who called out, "Hi, Marc."

Marc turned and looked in our direction. Our eyes locked. He said a few more words to his foreman, and then walked over to us.

"Hi, kids." He reached down and picked one up in each arm and snuggled them. They loved him without question.

That's how I loved him, too. From then on, if he'd let me, I'd show him that love and let him know that was more important than anything else.

He set the kids down and looked at me. "Maria," he said quietly.

"I've missed you. I called, but—"

He nodded. "Yes, I know. I almost called back, but I had some thinking to do."

He was quiet for a minute. My heart pounded like a jackhammer out of control.

Then he smiled. "That's when I realized you mean more to me than anything."

I put my hand on his arm. "Marc, you are my life. I'm sorry I couldn't see that before. Everything you've said is true."

He put his arm around me. "We'll work all this out together. That is, if you'll let me help you."

It was my turn to smile. "Yes, Marc, I want your help. You'll never know how much."

Several months have passed. Marc and I were married in a small ceremony with only our families present. Eva and Brendan will soon be our children legally. They haven't asked about their mother lately. Someday, I hope they'll know how much she loved them.

Marsha is the same. I visit her once or twice a week. The children go with me once a month. I want them to remember their mother.

Al's trial finally took place. He was convicted and sentenced to twenty years in prison. He's appealing, of course, but I know now there's nothing more I can do.

My father is being well taken care of, in the same nursing home as Marsha, although another unit. I visit him when I see Marsha. Neither of them recognizes me.

Sadly, Mom passed away recently, but not before she saw me marry Marc. The smile on her face at the ceremony is locked in my memory.

I look outside and see Marc playing ball with Brendan and Eva. We plan on having more children in a few years. I know now that life isn't perfect, but I'm thankful for the many wonderful times there are and plan on savoring them in the future.

THE END

MY UNFAITHFUL HEART
My kindness and love
destroyed three lives

My sister, Felicia, was two years younger than I. Even though we had similar coloring, Daddy said she looked just like my beautiful mother. Mom had died when Felicia was born. Felicia had that special spark that set her apart from others.

I adored her, and so did my father. She was our darling, the shining star of our lives. There were no rules for Felicia, no denials. After my mother died, I took over many of the household chores. I got good grades in school. Felicia didn't get good grades, but nobody minded.

She'd hand her report card to Daddy and toss herself into his lap nuzzling against his neck. "I tried," she'd purr. "Honest. But it's so stupid."

Daddy would try to be stern, but he couldn't do it. He was always seeing my mother in Felicia, I guess.

"I'll help you, Felicia," I'd say eagerly.

"Okay, Meredith," she'd say.

Of course, she never let me help her. She'd continue to float through life like an angel. Nothing bad ever happened to Felicia. Sometimes, she'd see something she'd like, so she'd just take it. I would return the item so Felicia wouldn't get into trouble.

Felicia was going to be a great ballerina. We'd lie in bed, and she'd talk about a big stage and all the eager audience, watching her in a costume, on her toes, spinning, spinning. I could hear that audience going crazy, clapping, shouting, calling her back again and again. I could see her taking bows.

But sometimes she would skip her dancing lesson. "Mrs. Yageshi is just a hick," she'd say. "I want to study under a great teacher. I know more than Mrs. Yageshi."

So we lived our lives. Felicia, beautiful and talented—my father, gentle with sadness always far back in his eyes—and me trying to make life easy for Felicia and do the little things for Daddy that Mother might have done.

Then tragedy struck. We dashed out of our room, heading for the steep stairwell. Felicia gave me a friendly little shove, pushing me off balance. I stumbled over a table and bounced back against her. She swayed, and despite my frantic lunge for her, toppled down the stairs. Her scream shot through me like a knife. There was a dreadful thumping, and then utter stillness.

I scrambled down the stairs and bent over her. Then Ruth, our housekeeper, came. Later the doctor arrived, and they took her to the hospital.

When they brought Felicia home, weeks later, we knew that she was paralyzed from the waist down. She would never be a great ballerina now. Felicia would never walk or run or dance again.

I could not bear the hurt in my father's eyes or the lost look on Felicia's pale face. I had done this to her. It was my fault!

I knelt by her bed and cried. Then I felt her hand on my hair. "Don't cry, Meredith," she said. "It wasn't really your fault. I should have remembered how clumsy you are."

My father stood in the doorway, his face stern. "Meredith, we'll have no more crying."

I crept out of the room. After that, I only cried when I was alone. They made a bedroom out of the downstairs den. It was a new, dreadful life.

Daddy worked harder than ever, because of the hospital and doctor bills. His face was gray, and he only smiled when he was with Felicia. He'd joke with her, tease her a little, and bring her small luxuries. But when he'd walk out of her room, the grayness would be back.

At first, I could hardly force myself to go into that room. And then one day, Felicia looked straight at me and spoke. "Meredith, I love you. Hurry home from school and talk to me."

"How about bringing some of the kids home with me?" I asked as my voice quivered.

Her lips trembled. "No," she said. "I'm just a—nothing now. I won't see anyone. I won't!"

I spoke to Daddy about it. It took courage to speak to him those days, because his eyes always avoided mine. "Don't force her," he said. "Give her time. Do whatever she wants."

So time went on. My life revolved around that downstairs bedroom and my sister, whom I had almost destroyed. People came to the house, bringing flowers and gifts, but Felicia would see no one. She was like a wounded bird that must hide. After awhile, people stopped coming.

One day they took Felicia away to the hospital again and operated. My hopes for her were deep prayers. She just had to walk again! I thought I couldn't take any more guilt.

They brought her home. "She should be able to walk. I don't understand it," the specialist told Daddy. Then he went into Felicia's room and I heard his voice, gentle asking her to try.

20

I heard her wail, "I can't, I can't! Stop torturing me."

Daddy never spoke about it again. So Felicia never tried, and we didn't encourage her. The specialist told Daddy that we shouldn't let her give up, but Daddy didn't have the heart to do it. A few weeks later, a wheelchair arrived for Felicia. Then I knew my beautiful sister would never walk again.

After school, I'd lift her into it and wheel her into the living room. I suggested that she get schooled at home, but she didn't see the point. She wasn't going to go anywhere, so what did she need classes about algebra and chemistry for?"

"But, the more you know, the more you'll have to interest you. You mustn't stop growing."

She just looked up at me listlessly and my heart sank. Her eyes seemed to remind me that I was the one who had stopped her from dancing, who had left her life a blank. So I didn't press her.

I didn't go to college. After the medical bills, Daddy didn't have enough money. Plus, Felicia needed me. Someone had to care for her. I wouldn't leave her. She depended on me

One evening Daddy and I had a serious talk. His face was more worried than usual. "I'm carrying a large insurance policy, Meredith. In case anything happens to me, it's for Felicia."

I ached to put my arms around his stooped shoulders and hold him tight. But his eyes held me away from him. My guilt lay there between us, like a solid wall.

"You know I'll always stay with her," was all I said. "My life belongs to Felicia."

Six weeks later, Daddy was dead. He got pneumonia and didn't have enough resistance to fight it. I think he was glad to go. The torment of seeing Felicia was more than his tired heart could stand.

My young dreams of a home, husband, and babies died when my father did. I had to take care of Felicia by myself. I would never be able to do anything else because there was no one else.

Sometimes I'd think, "If only Felicia would complain! If only she'd be bitter, it would be easier for me." But she never did. She'd just follow me silently with those wide blue eyes of hers.

I never asked her to try to walk again, but I did persuade her to have a masseuse in once a week. It would help her circulation and make her more comfortable

One day the bank manager called me to say that I was spending a bit more than the investment of the insurance policy would cover. He suggested I sell the house and move into an apartment, but I refused. The house we'd grown up in was home to Felicia, a safe sanctuary from the world. I decided to let Ruth go. She had mentioned wanting to see her grandchildren more. She understood my dilemma and praised me for all I had done for Felicia. She also told me not to give up on life, that I needed to have one of my own.

"I know your father meant well, but it ain't right," she said, "for a young thing like you to be a slave. You deserve—"

I didn't let her finish. I just hugged her and thanked her for everything she'd done.

Taking care of the house and Felicia was hard work. I was exhausted every day, but I felt that it was the least that I could do. Felicia's food had to be dainty, to tempt her appetite, and I always had fresh flowers on the tray. Often just when I'd be in the middle of something she'd call me. But she was always so sweet about it that I'd try to push my fatigue out of sight.

"I'm lonely," she'd say. Or, "I miss you when I can't see you." Or, "Meredith, I hate to bother you, but the sun is in my eyes."

I used the time when the masseuse was with Felicia to run downtown for the shopping that could not be done over the phone.

"Did you have a nice time?" Felicia would ask when I got back, breathless from hurrying. "You should get out more, Meredith. Why don't you go to a movie once in awhile? I'll be all right. You shouldn't be tied down to a—"

"Don't," I'd beg her. "Felicia, don't. I want to be with you."

She'd smile and twist a strand of her lovely hair around her fingers.

Gradually Felicia got so she would push herself in her wheelchair a little. But she just did it to please me. She'd go from one end of the living room to the other, and then just sit there, looking helpless and lost. I tried so hard to get her interested in something, but my attempts failed.

"Put me in the county hospital," she said. "Then I won't be a bother to you. You're sick of me. I don't want to 'do things.' I could be happy if you'd stop nagging."

"Whatever she wants, Meredith, whatever she wants"—the old refrain kept running through my mind.

I put my arms around her. "You don't have to do anything you don't want to do. Not ever."

Months later, I had a small moment of hope, but it vanished like a broken bubble. Felicia was in her room in the wheelchair. I had pulled the shades up high to let in the sunshine but when I brought in her tea, the shade was down. My hands shook and the tea things rattled on the tray.

"Felicia," I whispered, "you stood up! You pulled that shade down. Oh, Felicia, how wonderful!"

Her eyes were clear and candid, and her smile was the saddest thing. "I'm sorry Meredith," she said. "You pulled it down yourself before you left the room. Oh, I'd like to be able to reach it." Her palms stroked helpless thighs of hers. "If I could move, I'd help you. You wouldn't have to work so hard."

"I don't mind the work, dear," I said. I must have forgotten lowering it. I remembered other incidents like this—a comb on the dresser instead of in the drawer, a bed jacket on a chair instead of at the foot of the bed. This was the same. It was just my desperate longing and hope that had played my imagination false.

Several times, I wanted to have the local doctor in to see Felicia. But she wouldn't let me. She'd cry, and her tears would leave me weak. "It's no use," she'd say. "He'll only torture me, like the others. Let's forget it."

Forget it! "Whatever she wants, whatever she wants!"

I was twenty-one when I met Kent Bailey. One day I went down to the bookstore to buy a crossword puzzle book. Felicia seemed to like them. It tired her to hold the pencil and the book, so I would read the words to her and write in the answers she gave. I'd always hated puzzles. We'd done so many that at night the silly words danced in my dreams. A two-letter word meaning mulberry . . . fabulous bird . . . Indian measure of weight.

As I hurried into the store, the new owner was closing up for the day. We looked at each other and all of a sudden, my heart gave a convulsive jump. I forgot that I'd long ago given up all hope of love and happiness.

He wasn't especially good-looking, but he a quick smile. I stammered a little asking for the book. And then we were talking as though we had known each other for years. For a moment, I even forgot Felicia.

As he wrapped the puzzle book, he said: "May I walk home with you?"

Lost in this new emotion, I said yes.

It wasn't until we reached the front steps that I remembered Felicia, who never wanted company. Felicia, was my special responsibility. My heart had been singing for the first time in years, but now it went dead and cold.

"Thank-you," I said abruptly. "I'd ask you in, but it's late."

Kent's eyes widened in surprise, but he smiled. "You'll be seeing me again, Meredith. I like the name. I like you."

I couldn't bear to look at him. "I'm pretty busy," I said.

"How about dinner tomorrow night?"

"Oh, I couldn't. Not possibly." I tried to smile, but my lips were beginning to quiver. I wished I hadn't met Kent. My dreams of love were better buried deep.

"We'll work it out," he said. "I'll see you soon."

I stood there on the steps for a moment fighting to control my feelings. Then I walked inside and down the hall to Felicia's room, at the rear of the house.

She was breathing rather fast, and her eyes searched my face. "Who was that?" she asked.

I managed to make my voice light. "What long ears you have, Grandma," I said—and was startled at the flush that crept up her throat.

"The windows are open," she reminded me.

"I was only teasing, Felicia. That was Kent Bailey, who bought out Salinger's bookstore. I guess he wanted my business, so he walked me home."

"What does he look like?" she asked, never taking her eyes off my face.

"Just average," I said, trying to be casual. "Nothing special. Here's the new book of crosswords. I'll get your supper now, and then we'll work a few."

But Felicia didn't want to work the puzzles. She just lay there, smiling that vague secret little smile of hers and staring up at the ceiling.

And me? Well, there isn't any way to tell how I felt. Excited but hopeless. Alive, as a woman should be, but wrapped in the old guilt.

A few days later, Felicia astounded me. "Look, Meredith, look!" she cried, excitement in her voice. "I can move my left leg a little!"

It was true! There wasn't much motion, but it was a miracle.

"You'll help me, Meredith?" she asked. "Help me to keep trying?"

I cried then, but Felicia just smiled.

After that she worked at it every day, and by the end of the week she was moving both legs. "I want to stand up all by myself," she announced then, and her eyes were shining. Very slowly, she slid those thin legs over the edge of the bed, sat up painfully. I was shaking with fear and hope.

Then triumphantly she was on her feet, swaying, laughing. "See, Meredith, see?" she cried.

I didn't question the timing because I was so happy. A week later, Kent Bailey caught up to me as I was hurrying home from the supermarket. Even through all the thrill of Felicia's miracle, he hadn't been out of my thoughts for a second. I welcomed just this small bit of heaven.

He touched my arm as I started up the steps. "Be kind to me," he said. "Talk to me awhile."

So Kent was lonely, too! A wild, irrational hope touched me. Now that Felicia was learning to walk, perhaps she would want to pick up her life again. My heart raced full tilt. Perhaps Felicia would even welcome the man I loved. I remembered her saying: "You should have a boyfriend, Meredith. You should go dancing."

But I had sense enough not to ask Kent in that day. We sat on the steps and talked in low voices. His shoulder brushed mine, and his eyes caressed me. I remember wondering what he could see in me. I reminded him that I lived with my ill sister. He surprised me and said he wanted to meet her.

When I went inside after leaving Kent, Felicia said: "You're late, Meredith. Did you meet that—what's his name, Kent Bailey?"

I felt my face turn crimson, so I fussed around, helping her into her nightgown. "He walked home with me," I admitted. "Felicia, maybe you'd like to meet him. He's interesting, and he's fun."

She lay there, her eyes wide on my face. I held my breath, waiting for her answer.

"Maybe sometime," she said. "If you want it, Meredith. If it will make you happy." She wanted to wait until she could stand without losing her balance. I was thrilled.

In the meantime, Kent would phone me evenings, and we'd talk and talk. Whenever I went downtown, we'd meet for a cup of coffee. But I never found the courage to tell him about Felicia's accident, about the load of guilt that I always carried with me. He walked me home that night and put his arms around his shoulders.

But even in that moment of exquisite happiness, I seemed to hear a voice calling from far away. A thin little voice that invaded our magic moment, that pulled me out of Kent's arms.

"It's Felicia," I whispered. "She's calling me."

Kent's face looked pale in the moonlight. "But there's so much I have to tell you, my darling."

"She's calling me," I repeated, and backed away from him toward the door. It was part habit, part guilt.

"You'll be right back?" he asked, and his eyes were puzzled.

I could hear her, the plaintive voice coming louder now. "Meredith, Meredith!"

"I'll see you tomorrow, Kent."

"Good night," he answered stiffly.

"Kent, please. You don't understand—"

But he was gone, striding down the street.

I leaned against the front door for a second, sick at heart. Then I walked into Felicia's room.

"You were so long out there," she said.

"You didn't need me?" I asked slowly.

"I always need you, Meredith." She laughed teasingly. "Your lipstick is smudged, dear. Meredith, I'd like to meet him, this Kent person. Invite him for dinner tomorrow."

My heart jumped, and I forgot that Felicia had smashed my precious moment. Kent would understand when I explained.

Right then I wanted to tell Felicia that Kent and I were in love, but some inner caution warned me not to move too fast She was like a yellow chick breaking out of its shell. I must be patient, let the future take care of itself.

"Of course I'll invite him," I told her

So that was how Kent met Felicia. I phoned him the next morning with Felicia sitting close by. I wanted to say "Darling, forgive me. It was wrong to leave you last night. Let me explain." Felicia was there, so I said simply, "My sister wants to meet you. She wants you for dinner tonight."

"Felicia wants me?" he said.

"You know I want you, too." As soon as I could talk to him alone, everything would be all right.

His voice was so odd. "Love me, love my sister—is that it?"

"I—I guess that's it."

"I accept," he said. "I'm looking forward to meeting Felicia."

I dressed Felicia carefully. I made sure her makeup was perfect and that she was comfortable before I dressed hurriedly. I smiled at Kent as I opened the door He smiled, too, but it wasn't the same. I took him to the dining room and introduced him to Felicia. He looked down at her, and she held out her hand in a shy delightful way. It there was a lightning bolt ripping through that room I wasn't aware of it. The man I loved was there—and my sister, whom I loved, was beginning to live again.

None of us talked much during dinner, but Felicia smiled often, and she was so beautiful that she didn't need to talk.

After coffee, she said in a small voice: "I'm just learning to walk again, Kent. I'm not very graceful, but don't mind. I'll learn."

He was around the table in a flash, and by her side.

She shook her head. "Let me do it al] by myself."

We stood there, Kent and I, and watched her push herself up, walk to a chair in the living room. Her laugh was young, excited. "See? I made it."

Kent said, "You're a very brave girl. I—I like a girl who knows what she wants and won't let anything interfere."

So that was the way it started, another tragedy. Only I didn't know that yet. I was blindly happy. Felicia was getting better, and I loved Kent Bailey. And Kent loved me. At least that's what I thought. I guess Kent did love me, for a little while. And maybe he would have continued if I hadn't insisted on sharing him with Felicia.

He came to the house often, bringing Felicia books and flowers. He and I were never alone together again. And then came the terrible evening, when I walked into the living room after doing the dinner dishes—and found Felicia and Kent clinging together in a tight embrace. My heart turned cold when I saw them.

So this was why Felicia had learned to walk again! I had lost Kent . . . lost him forever. I uttered a soft cry, and abruptly they broke apart.

Kent was the first to speak. "I'm sorry you had to find out this way," was all he said. He was embarrassed, flustered.

Not Felicia. She smiled at me. "Kent wants to be married right away. He doesn't mind about my disability," she said slowly.

My heart was numb and still. I couldn't answer.

"You don't want him, do you? I could tell if my own sister loved a man, couldn't I?"

"Yes," I said stiffly. "You could tell Felicia. I'm happy for you. Terribly happy, dear."

Somehow, I managed to get out of the room, to be alone, nursing my hurt, feeling my heart crumble. Felicia deserved her happiness. This was part of my atonement for the past. They planned to be married quietly at home.

"Where will you live?" I asked.

Felicia said, "Why, here, of course."

"Then I'll find a small apartment."

"Meredith!" Felicia's voice held a hint of tears. "This is our home, yours and mine, and now Kent's. I couldn't live without you."

I thought of all the little things that Felicia still me to do for her. What difference would it make to me now? I was so dead inside that watching the two of them together couldn't hurt me.

"All right. If Kent doesn't mind, I'll stay."

"Mind?" Kent said. "Why should I? I'll be delighted."

Later, he caught up to me in the hall. "You knew I'd fall in love with her, didn't you? What man wouldn't? You're cold, Meredith—to everyone but Felicia. It's an obsession with you, heaven knows why."

It was too late for telling Kent the truth now, but my pride was saved. My heart was dead. I even managed to laugh.

They were married in front of our fireplace, Felicia a dream bride in misty white chiffon. Kent took Felicia to the doctor, over her protests, for a general checkup. The doctor said she was remarkably strong, considering the years she had lain in bed. It was incredible that her muscles still worked. She would walk with a slight limp, but otherwise she was physically perfect.

When Kent told me the good news, I explained about her wanting to be a ballerina. He told me that life was a compromise and that she should be happy with all she could still do.

I wondered if Felicia would tell Kent about the accident, but she didn't. It was agonizing for me to watch Felicia with the man I loved. I knew I would have to bear the burden for hurting her forever.

We'd played three-handed card games, and I'd have to watch Felicia cuddle in his lap. Sometimes, I'd just knit while they talked about their day. I tried to keep a smile on my face, but it was difficult. Then I'd watch him carry her to their room as he whispered in her ear. She'd giggle, then kiss him softly. I tried to keep out of their way.

My routine was the same as before Kent married Felicia. I did the housework, the laundry, the cooking. Kent assumed that Felicia and I shared the work, and neither of us told him otherwise. But Felicia trailed around, arranging flowers, brushing her hair, and doing her nails. At four, I always had her lie down so she'd be fresh when Kent came home. Perhaps I was deliberately twisting the knife, playing the martyr. My mind was coiled in a tight spiral that kept me from seeing life straight. But I was to see—and soon.

Felicia was forever talking about Kent. "He's a wonderful lover," she'd say, her eyes on my face. "So gentle, so fierce." Bitterly I remembered Kent's kisses that night when a thin, plaintive voice had pulled me out of his arms.

"Meredith, you should be married," Felicia announced one day.

"I don't want a husband," I said, and heard my voice shake.

"But you must be lonely," she insisted. That opaque look was in her eyes, and she was smiling.

Kent got a vacation in June, and they went on their delayed honeymoon. Felicia wanted me to go along. "I need Meredith," she insisted. "She knows how to rub my head when it aches. She does my hair." She switched to bright laughter. "We'll find her a husband, Kent."

"That's enough nonsense," I interrupted. "You can get along without me perfectly well, and you know it. I—I'll be glad to be alone for a change."

Felicia looked hurt, but I didn't care. I had to be alone to rebuild my courage, and she had to learn to live without me as a cushion against life. It was the first time that I realized that Felicia's continued dependence upon me wasn't necessary. Later, I was to realize much more.

They went on their trip, and the house was quiet and haunted by ghosts. For two weeks, I fought myself, praying for peace. And I thought I found peace of a sort. But I had only pushed the torment down deeper, where I could pretend it did not exist. That only banked the agony of the fires, kept them smoldering.

Then Felicia and Kent returned. It wasn't until Kent left for the store the next morning that I noticed the strange look about Felicia. I took in her breakfast tray as usual about ten, but she pushed it aside.

Her face was white, and there were small drops of moisture on her forehead and along her upper lip.

"What's wrong, darling?" I asked her.

"I'm pregnant," she said, and her voice was childishly flat. "I don't want a baby, Meredith. I don't want to be ugly. I don't even like babies."

For the first time, a definite dreadful suspicion touched me. I looked at Felicia, and stark fright was in her eyes.

"Meredith, darling, you've always taken care of me," she said. "Take care of me now. Take me to someone who will get rid of this. I'm not strong." Her voice rose. "I'll die, Meredith. I don't want to die!"

Small memories came back to haunt me, little things, which I had ignored at the time, but which had piled up into a heap against the stonewall of my blindness. Now, however, I had no time for memories.

"You can't destroy the baby, Felicia. If the doctor says it isn't safe for you to have a baby, we'll abide by that. But babies are part of marriage and a miracle. You'll love yours when it comes."

"No!" she screamed. "I won't have it! I don't want Kent's baby. Help me, Meredith. You promised to look after me. You promised!"

Pity and disgust writhed inside me. Then the door swung wide and Kent stood there. His face was crumpled. He looked very, very tired. "I came back for a book," he said tonelessly. "I heard."

The fright was still with Felicia, and I knew then that she had never loved Kent. "You've tricked me," she told him, crying. "Help me, Kent, help me!"

The silence was a deep, mourning thing. "Meredith is right. We'll abide by what the doctor says." He set his chin, and seemed to compose himself with an effort. "We'll discuss the rest—later."

Felicia wept and pleaded, and there was childish yet fierce anger threaded through it all. But Kent phoned the doctor.

When he'd hung up, she drew a long breath and closed her eyes. "I'm tired. Forgive me Meredith, Kent." A tiny smile touched her lips. "I guess a little baby will be nice. I want to sleep now."

Kent and I sat in the living room, not talking, until the doctor came to see Felicia. I think Kent was too stunned to speak. As for me, my brain was racing over the past, and everything that had happened was like a jigsaw puzzle that after weeks of effort suddenly begins to fall into place.

Perhaps I should have told the doctor what Felicia had said, how she had acted. But I didn't—and later that was to add to the guilt feeling piling up in my confused, tortured mind.

The doctor assured us that Felicia was in good shape and

shouldn't have any trouble with her pregnancy.

He went away, and I looked at Kent. "It's my fault," I whispered. "I kept her a child. Don't worry, Kent. She'll accept the baby, learn to love it."

His eyes did not meet mine. "I'll move across the hall to the den," he said. He tried to smile. "Perhaps this is part of the business of having a baby. The upset emotions, the resentment."

"Of course it is," I said. But I knew better.

Felicia slept until late afternoon when I woke her. "Here's tea and cinnamon toast, dear," I said. "You haven't eaten all day."

I tried to make my voice natural, but Felicia's dreadful desire to be rid of the baby had brought to the surface all those nagging past memories. Suddenly I thought of the pulled-down shade, when she hadn't been able to walk. Perhaps she had been able to walk. Perhaps she had been walking for months and months. Then there was the night Kent had been kissing me. Things were becoming serious between us, but she called me. Maybe she had done it on purpose. I just hadn't wanted to accept it, yet.

I set the tray down. "Thank you, Meredith," she said in a small, subdued voice.

"You were upset this morning, Felicia. Let's forget it. You're going to have a beautiful baby, and you and Kent are going to be proud and happy."

She just looked at me and smiled. Again, I should have been warned. I was confused and in shock. As I picked up the tray, something clattered to the floor. I stooped and picked up a slim steel knitting needle.

"That's yours," Felicia said quickly. "You left it there."

"How absentminded I'm getting," I said.

Her smile widened a bit, and there was that queer look far back in her eyes. "You must teach me to knit little booties," she said.

The next few days were very tense. Kent came home, but barely spoke to either of us. His eyes always looked sad and pleading. He seemed as though he wanted to talk to me, but he couldn't manage to get out the words.

*Felicia stayed in bed, though the doctor had told her to live normally. "I'll get up soon," she'd say. "Maybe tomorrow." She let me bring her food, but usually she wanted to be alone. I felt as though a great black cloud was pressing down on us, yet I couldn't stop it.

And then about three o'clock one morning I wakened to the sound of a high scream. Kent got to Felicia's room ahead of me lifted her from the floor, laid her on her bed. Her screams ripped at the air even as he phoned the doctor.

Perhaps I suspected at that moment. Then she started talking through the screams. She was delirious, of course, and I hoped that Kent believed it was only pain and fever. But for me it was the truth coming out, confirming all my half-formed suspicions.

"Meredith . . . Kent," she said, almost moaning out the words. "Look what you've done to me. Meredith crippled me, and now this!" Crazy laughter mixed with a scream of pain. "But I got my revenge, didn't I, Meredith? All those years you thought I couldn't walk. You stayed home and waited on me. And then Kent. I took him away from you. It was almost too easy to be fun. He's such a stupid man. You're stupid, too, Meredith."

She lay still for a moment, breathing loudly. "Was it fun, Meredith, watching Kent and me together? Was it fun, was it fun?"

So now it was all in the open—the hate Felicia had been nursing for years, the clever way she had tormented me, fooled me with her sweet smile.

"She's delirious," I told Kent. "She doesn't know what she's saying."

I sat down on the edge of the bed, and I didn't hate her. It was my entire fault. "What's wrong, Felicia? What's happened?" I asked.

"I don't know. I haven't done anything. Help me, Meredith, help me!"

"Try to lie still, darling. The doctor will be right here."

Kent looked at me, his face distraught. "You heard what she said, didn't you?" he cried. "Are you a saint? Haven't you any human emotions?"

"Never mind," I said. "I told you it was delirium."

Felicia's hands clawed at me desperately. We rushed her to the hospital. The doctor came out of the emergency room. "She's lost the baby, and I'm not sure I can save her."

Still trying to protect her, I asked: "A miscarriage?"

"No," was his answer. "Self-induced abortion. She denies it, but it's plain."

The awful guilt washed over me. Why hadn't I watched her? Why hadn't I realized she was living a lie, hating me, hating Kent, hating the idea of a baby? Felicia had refused to grow up because it was easier to stay a child.

What do you do, how do you feel, when the earth crumbles beneath your feet? What do you say when you know that by your efforts to atone for an accident you have turned your sister into this?

Kent was looking at me and his eyes were full of a sick horror.

"She's only a child, Kent," I said. "She didn't know any better. You mustn't blame her."

Slowly, softly he said: "She knew better. She just didn't care."

Felicia died that night. I did all the things that had to be done.

31

Kent helped, too, but we didn't look at each other. There was a wall between us. I realized that I had to get away. I had to get away from the memories and Kent I packed Felicia's clothes and sent them away. I sold the house. Then I bought a ticket to a big city a hundred and fifty miles away.

Kent drove me to the station. "Meredith, Meredith," he said, "there's so much to be cleared up between us. So much to talk about."

"There's nothing," I answered. "The past belongs to me."

"Must you go?" His voice was soft.

"There's nothing to stay for," I told him. "Just ghosts. I can't live with ghosts." I looked at him and he was a stranger. Once I had loved him, and he had married Felicia. Now there was nothing, because of the numb shock. I supposed he was suffering, grieving, too. Yet, I couldn't share his grief.

."If only you'd cry, Meredith," he said.

"Why should I cry?" I heard myself laugh, and it was a small, impatient sound.

"Let me know where you are, Meredith. Promise."

It was two weeks later that the anesthesia of shock wore off, and I fell apart. I couldn't stop crying for a few days. Somehow I crawled into a taxi and got back to my apartment.

Perhaps, the crying that saved me. This time I was not fighting for a false peace. With my tears, the past washed to the surface, like seaweed drifting upward. It was there and I faced it—and saw I straight. It was more Felicia's fault that mine that she had plummeted down thou stairs. The memories hurt, but facing them gave me a slow release from the guilt.

I could hear again the sound of Felicia's voice screaming her hate at me. I destroyed my sister by patience, devotion, and kindness. And I destroyed myself by not giving my love to the man who wanted it. I let my unfaithful heart destroy Felicia, Kent, and me.

Daddy had said: "Whatever she wants, whatever she wants." And I had done what I had done with love, with the best that was in me. Felicia's pattern of behavior had been set long before the accident. Daddy had also loved her too much.

Kent? I had sinned against him unknowingly, too, pushed his love aside at the moment when his heart was most vulnerable. I knew now that I still loved him, that I would always love him. Whether he still loved me or not, I couldn't know. Only the gentleness of time would wipe away the scars, perhaps give us another chance.

I enrolled in a nursing program and walked nights to pay the bills. I still had money left from the sale of the house, but I didn't want to touch it. It seemed like blood money. Finally, I realized that I needed to go back if I wanted to have a peaceful future.

At the end of the first year, I got a vacation. I went back home. I needed to get rid of all the ghosts. I cried a little, watching the children playing in the sandbox in the yard. But the tears were part pleasure. At last, the house was a home for happiness, for real living.

Then I drove downtown toward Kent's bookstore, my heart trembling as eagerly as on the night he first kissed me. Would he be there? Would he be happy to see me? Had he erased the past, as I had?

Minutes later, my heart had the answer to all those questions. I was in Kent's arms, and we were clinging tightly together, lost in the delirious joy of having found each other again.

"Meredith, Meredith, it's been too long. Much too long," he murmured against my ear. I nodded, and my heart raced exultantly inside me as I lifted my face for his kiss. It was the end of ugly memories, old scars. Now I could begin life again. And Kent and I could share it together.

THE END

MY SISTER:
SAINT, OR—SADIST?
They say truth sets you free, but
I'm so afraid to know. . . .

When my sister emailed me to announce her visit, my chest filled with warmth and pride—because my sister was no ordinary person: Natascha was a saint.

For three decades, she selflessly gave six months out of every year to help AIDS victims in Africa. Journalists hailed her as "The Angel of Uganda."

She was an angel to me, too, my personal guardian angel—the only source of kindness and support I ever had throughout our desolate childhoods.

Our father turned our family home into a torture chamber, treating us children as objects for his sadistic pleasures. I had a rusty nail hammered through my kneecap; Natascha got her big toe smashed with a mallet.

"An accident," my father would explain. "You know how careless children can be."

Teachers, neighbors, and the priests we knew accepted the "accidents" with indifference and shrugged off our tears. My mother, passive and frightened, did little to protect us. She fed us three meals a day and ignored us otherwise.

Natascha alone, my older sister, took an interest in me. She taught me to read, to write little stories, and to say a few sentences in French and Spanish. Her kindness was like a strip of sunlight falling through a narrow slit into a dark cell. I worshipped her as a child, and I continued to worship her through my adult years—albeit, from a distance. A photo of the two of us clinging together—she at sixteen and me at seven—stood, silver-framed, on my mantel.

Then at seventeen, Natascha ran away. She simply left home one day without warning—without even saying good-bye to me. For two years I heard nothing from her and after awhile, I knew that she might very well be dead, although I admit I always felt keenly that she was alive somewhere, hiding.

Meanwhile, with Natascha gone, I was left to bear the brunt of our father's violent brutality and sadistic cruelty. It wasn't until I turned nineteen that I finally managed to extricate myself from his claws by finding a job several states away.

Later, I found out that Natascha went to California, working first as a chambermaid and later training as a nurse. I moved to Maine, where I became an office assistant. In a way, I guess we both put as big a distance between our unhappy childhood home in Louisiana and ourselves as we could—geographically speaking, at least. Indeed, with the whole continent between us and both of us struggling financially, it was difficult for us to arrange meetings. In fact, for twenty years, we didn't meet up—not even once.

Oh, we corresponded, of course, and she sent me press clippings and told me of the TV documentaries about her charitable work that aired regularly on Public Television. I also followed her brave, selfless actions as reported and profiled on the Internet. Sometimes we tried to meet, but it never worked out. Natascha always had to cancel, and I must admit that I understood. With half of every year dedicated to her charity work, and the other half to working full-time as a nurse and raising funds for her Uganda project, I knew my sister had little free time, and certainly no money left over to fly out to Maine.

So you can certainly understand that I was surprised and thrilled when she finally emailed me about a visit. I rushed to cancel all of my commitments for that week, hired a cleaner, stocked up on health foods, and the fair-trade coffees and herbal teas that I know she prefers. Then I looked around my flat and tried to see it through her eyes, thinking: Conventional . . . will she find it bourgeois? The ethnic wall rugs in warm, bright colors—I never investigated their origins and suddenly I felt guilty about that, wondering, What if children working eighteen hours a day in a sweatshop in Pakistan made them? And my laptop computer—will Natascha disdain the luxury of modern technology in a private home?

Natascha always maintained that all she needed to live was one straw mat, one blanket, and one change of clothing. I tried not to feel embarrassed about my bulging wardrobe and cozy bed. Those things don't really matter, though, I assured myself. Natascha's an angel, a saint, and surely she'll understand and tolerate my own lifestyle, even if it doesn't necessarily meet up to her rigid standards.

After all, I considered, it's my friendship and sisterly support that she's seeking while her world is falling apart. You see, as it was, the hospital where Natascha had worked for a decade had been taken over, and the new employers objected to the unusual terms of her contract that allowed her several months unpaid leave each year. Since, she'd applied for jobs with one hospital, one clinic, and one institution after another—and they all turned her down. Her many years of varied experience, her solid qualifications as a registered nurse, her hardworking attitude—all of these wonderful attributes suddenly seemed to count for nothing. Natascha was nearing fifty, and they preferred younger nurses.

To make matters worse, Natascha couldn't even show a school leaving certificate—my father saw to that. While we were growing up, he held us back in school, usually by calling us in as "sick." Well, of course we were "sick"—after he stomped his boots into our bellies.

For most of her career, Natascha's nursing qualifications were sufficient, and her employers never asked for anything more. But suddenly, it seemed, all of her fellow jobseekers had advanced degrees.

Needless to say, Natascha was bewildered and angry about being dismissed from her job after so many years—and even more so due to the all-too-evident ageism she suddenly encountered in the job market. She needed someone to talk to, someone who understood—and who better than her own sister? I know she also hoped that the state of Maine might prove less ageist than California, or at least offer more employment opportunities for experienced nursing staff.

Of course I instantly agreed to her visit. I cancelled all of my own plans for that week and made an immediate start on her translation work. After all those many years, I felt I finally had a chance to repay my sister for at least some of the kindness Natascha showed me while we growing up. As it was, I marveled that Natascha, who certainly endured the same loveless, tortured childhood that I did, developed into such a wonderful person, so sane and saintly. I knew all too well that she might very well have become emotionally damaged—perhaps even as cruel as our father, or as meek and cowardly as our mother. Instead, she became this strong, brave, compassionate woman.

Of course I've turned out all right, too—in my own modest way. Deprived of proper schooling and the opportunity to go to college, I made up for these inherent disadvantages by educating myself as best as I could and attending night school and online courses. I learned languages and secretarial skills and I even achieved a postgraduate diploma as a mature student. The certificate for that hangs, proudly framed, amidst all of the other certificates I've collected over the years; in fact, a whole wall in my living room is dedicated to certificates, a proud reminder that despite the odds and my father's intended sabotage, I've been able to achieve.

Still, compared with Natascha, I never thought I was anything special. Natascha's the one who achieved real meaning in her life. Her compassion and energy made real differences not only for AIDS victims, but for landmine victims and in light of such self-sacrifice—what's a wall full of certificate, compared with a tally of lives and limbs saved?

When Natascha alighted from the train, I found her little changed from the photos she sent me a decade ago: about my height, skinny where I'm overweight, her hair pulled back into a tight bun. We hugged and nearly danced on the platform with the joy of our reunion.

In the evening, we sat—she, cross-legged on my Peruvian rug while I curled up in my settee—and swapped reminiscences, not to mention all of those memories too painful to share with an "outsider."

Natascha's raw voice revealed how fresh the horrors still were in her mind, even after so many years. "And then he threw me on the bed, his face red with rage while he slapped me over and over again. Then he—he kicked me in the stomach, ripped my blouse open . . . he started grabbing and clawing at my breasts. . . ."

With clenched teeth, I closed my eyes. Even so, I saw the scene, vivid before my eyes. I could feel the man's bulk, smell the stale sweat, the hint of mothballs in his clothes. That beast—our flesh-and-blood father—did similar things to me.

Then I brought up the subject of how she taught me reading and writing, and helped me to write little compositions for school. "You know, Nat—that's the best thing that happened to me in all my life," I told her earnestly.

She shifted on the rug. "Did I really? I mean—did I really do all of those things—for you?"

I was disappointed that she didn't remember these crucial—nay, critical—times. True, even I only remember a handful of afternoons that we actually spent together—she the superior teacher, I the willing pupil, eagerly absorbing it all. But surely, I thought, there must've been many such afternoons through all the years of our childhood, even if even I can't recall all of them.

She pondered. "Of course I remember I had to do some babysitting and minding. Mum always made me. So I guess I probably taught you writing then. After all, there wasn't exactly much else I could do with you. You were always such a dull child, so withdrawn."

I gulped, thinking suddenly, Strange that Natascha's not only half-forgotten those precious hours, but that she regarded them as times filled with little more than dull chores put upon her by our put-upon mother. Still, I decided, that doesn't make them any less valuable to me. Mentally, I added "pure honesty" to the list of what I perceived as my big sister's "saintly" attributes.

Natascha declined the herbal tea I offered, but accepted a bottle of wine, declaring: "We have to celebrate!" By the end of the evening, she was mildly drunk.

She talked about her project—the nonprofit organization she launched and maintained to help AIDS sufferers and orphans, and how she raised funds. "Of course I didn't really want to sleep with him, but he'd already donated 20,000 Euros to the project and he was offering me 100,000 more."

I blinked, startled, hoping I'd misheard her. "You mean—you

had sex with him just because he gave you money for the project?" I asked carefully.

She must've heard the disapproval in my voice. "Oh, don't be such a prude," she spat. "And for once in your life—stop being so damned judgmental!"

I swallowed hard, all the while thinking, "Saints" don't prostitute themselves—not even to raise funds for a worthy cause. Then I asked, "Do you sleep with all of your sponsors?"

"Of course not. I'm not a whore, for Pete's sake!" She sounded outraged. "And most sponsors donate much smaller amounts, anyway."

Confused, I brought the conversation to an end. For a couple of hours afterward, we studied the "employment opportunity" advertisements in the local newspapers. As it was, our town's hospital was recruiting qualified staff; they might or might not be prepared to employ a nurse on a "six-months-per-year" basis, but I figured it was worth inquiring about. A private care home for elderly invalids also had vacancies for temporary caregivers, and I thought that might be another option for Natascha.

"I would certainly love having you in the neighborhood," I added as a hopeful incentive. Then I made sure that she was comfortable for the night and withdrew to sleep.

The next day we went walking in the woods, where the only sounds were whispers of the wind in the treetops, and the occasional screech of a bird of prey. Wild mushrooms beckoned on the rabbit-grazed meadows and Natascha squealed with delight like a child discovering a lost-and-found toy.

"Parasols!" she exclaimed. "I haven't picked mushrooms in years!"

At the sight of my sister's happiness, my chest filled with warm pride. If she gets a job in Maine, I mused hopefully, we'll be able to spend many weekends together just like this. I took several photos of her harvesting mushrooms with my little digital camera—a cheap, secondhand item I bought on eBay.

Natascha asked to examine it. "I'm planning to buy a digital camera myself soon," she explained. "But something with more memory, better resolution, and a higher optical zoom."

"You'll have to wait until you have a job and you're earning money again," I replied innocently enough.

She laughed—a kind of derisive snorting sound. "Heck no! I'll just use the project money, like I always do. After all, there's certainly plenty in the landmine aid account right now."

My jaw dropped and I felt my eyes widen in shocked disbelief. "The project money?" I repeated, stunned. "You mean—you just— take the money that's been donated for the cause . . . and buy things for yourself?"

She shrugged, looking just as nonchalant and nonplussed as could be. "Well, you know—I've certainly worked hard enough for the project; I've worked my ass off, in fact. So they owe me something, at least—wouldn't say? Besides, I'm the one who raised most of the funds in the first place."

I remembered the fundraising method she'd mentioned the night before. "But—don't you have to account for all of the money?"

She gave another snort, smirking at me like I was the biggest rube she ever met. "Sure. But I can always very easily 'justify' that I 'need' a digital camera for 'documentation purposes.'"

On the way home, we stopped in at a café for lattes, but I was silent. "Saints," I couldn't help thinking over and over, even hardworking ones, don't divert funds from charitable projects.

Then I wondered: But am I being too judgmental, too . . . 'conventional?' I remember Natascha called me those things years ago, back when I was too young to even fully grasp their meaning.

Maybe I should unbend a little, I decided then. After all, Natascha's undoubtedly one of the heroes of the modern world. And if she's less than perfect, well, then . . . maybe I expected too much, putting her on a pedestal and worshipping her from afar. After all, she's certainly wonderful, but she's also only human. She's a normal human being with flaws.

In the evening, I uncorked another bottle of wine. I hoped to talk about the depression that had nearly knocked the life out of me five years earlier. I wanted to tell Natascha what I was never able to tell anyone else—about how I'd kidded myself all those years, choosing to believe that I'd somehow "survived" my childhood unscathed and then how, five years ago, the memories suddenly unfolded and hit me with all of the power of a lightning strike.

But suddenly, I found myself hesitating about sharing this intimate secret with her. Instead, I listened to her enthuse about her current lover, a Greek, twenty years her junior. Wishing to remain faithful to his wife, he'd initially resisted Natascha's seduction for a long time. But, Natascha told me with a satisfied smirk, she "got him in the end," and now he was practically "addicted" to her.

"Anyway, I don't really fancy him," she said. "But at my age, I feel like I need the sex boost."

Her attitude caused a sick feeling in my stomach. By my standards, seducing a married man is a sin, but I knew there was no point in bringing this up to my sister. I figured she'd merely dismiss me as "prudish and judgmental."

Then suddenly, an incident came to my mind. I remembered then that when I was six, Natascha helped herself to my cherished crayons and used them up, leaving me with only the tiny, peeled-down stumps.

When I protested, she accused me of being "unsisterly," selfish, and mean-spirited. She made me feel that she was entirely in the right, while I was entirely in the wrong.

The more I thought, the more I found that other long-forgotten incidents began to resurface in my mind. My pretty, silk scarf that she cut up to use for an appliqué cushion . . . the tiny china doll I bought at a garage sale with my babysitting money—and that she decided made "the perfect gift" for her best friend's birthday party. . . .

Suddenly, I felt uneasy at the prospect of having her live nearby, wondering, even as a strange, cold sheen of anxious, unnerved perspiration covered me, Will she require me to recommend her to employers and landlords? Can I even do that with a clear conscience? After all, now that I really think about it—how much do I really know about her . . . and how much of what I think I know about her is really the hazy, childish, nostalgic memories of yesteryear, or ill-conceived perceptions based on little more than wishful thinking?

In the morning, when I entered the living room with plates of fried eggs, Canadian bacon, and buttered rye toast, I found her studying my framed diplomas.

"You're really proud of these, aren't you?"

There was a gleam in her eye that I mistook for enthusiasm. I put the plates down on the glass-topped coffee table and poured coffee for each of us as I told her about how I'd educated myself, at first secretly, so that my father wouldn't find out—mostly in my bed at night, with a flashlight under the quilt. I talked about the night courses I took and all of the online courses, and all of the exams I passed—and even aced.

She curled her upper lip, studying me acutely. "Do these pieces of paper make you a better person?"

"No, of course not," I replied, taken aback. "But they are proof of my achievements—of how I've made my way in the world, even though our—" I refused to speak the word "father." "Even though—he—tried to prevent us from finding any senses of joy and self-worth."

"So you hang up certificates, then—so that you can celebrate yourself." She snorted. "A whole wall full of them. Jeez. What a pathetic creature you turned out to be—that you need these 'bits of paper; to prop up your confidence and keep you from sinking into the gutter!"

For several long minutes, I found myself at a complete and utter loss over what to say. Then I swallowed my hurt and looked her plainly in the eyes. "Look, Natascha—this is my home, and I've chosen to display my certificates. If you don't like them, then simply don't look at them. Now, let's have breakfast. The eggs are getting cold."

She lifted one of the frames off the wall—the gold-colored one that contains my postgraduate diploma. "All these years—and this is all you have to show for it?"

Anger burned in my chest, mingled with pain. The hand with which I clutched my coffee cup trembled and all of a sudden I felt disoriented—like I'd gone for a long walk in unfamiliar woods and lost my way.

What is this about? I wondered, finding myself crushed and baffled all at once. Why is my beloved sister trying to hurt me?

While I half-listened to Natascha's tirades and accusations—cruel comments that came faster than I could answer them, anyway—memories, dark memories from our shared past, awoke in my mind. . . .

I looked in her eyes, and all at once . . . I recognized the expression: It was the look of a hawk hovering over its chosen prey.

It was the look in our father's eyes after he delivered a punch to my stomach, watching me recover from the pain and nausea before he delivered the second blow that would rob me of my balance and breath.

And then it all became clear . . . like a mirror with the mist wiped clean.

I remembered then—those days when Natascha was kind to me. . . . Oh, but, truth be told—those times were really very rare, I began to realize. She was only kind to me after our father humiliated me. That's when she used to take me for walks, teach me things, show me kindness. . . . But that kindness never lasted long—only ever for a couple of days, at most. And then I'd pay for those brief times of kindness; usually after the second day, she turned to hurting me, getting crueler by the moment. Then she'd belittle me, humiliate me. She always did that to make herself feel greater and more powerful than shrimpy, little me. . . .

I realized then that somewhere along the way, somehow through the years, I'd chosen—consciously or unconsciously—to forget all that, to look back on those awful times and remember only those brief, fleeting moments of kindness and caring.

I suppose I simply desperately needed to believe that there was at least someone in my family who was lovable, admirable. So I built up Natascha. I idealized her, idolized her—shaped her image into that of a saint and placed her up high above me on a pedestal. I simply refused to see Natascha for the toxic, self-centered, selfish person she truly is.

All those years, I began to realize, she never needed me. But now . . . now she's come . . . not because she wants to make contact and reconnect with her long-lost sister—not even because she wants my emotional support. She's come to me simply because she's been

41

humiliated . . . and now she needs someone to torment and humiliate in order to make herself feel great again.

And me—just look at me! I fell right into her trap again—just like I did when I was just a defenseless, little girl who craved love and affection.

And Natascha—she hasn't changed. Not one single bit. She still uses the same old tricks to fulfill her immature needs.

But I've changed.

Despite years of denial followed by years of depression, somehow, along the way, I've learned to value myself. I've achieved the education I strove for; I have a career I cherish that truly enriches every aspect of my life. I've finally gained that almighty "approval" from friends, coworkers, and employers.

I don't need Natascha's validation anymore.

I raised my chin. "Leave," I told her then. "Get out and don't come back."

She stared at me—the same surprised stare that our father gave me when one day, I finally told him to get out of my life, and stay out of it for good. Then she laughed—the same disbelieving, derisive laugh.

"You'll call me back. You need me. I'm your sister."

I opened the door. I was crying then, but at the same time, I was smiling.

Because I knew she was mistaken.

Years ago I finally cut my father from my life—and I have never regretted it. I have never allowed him back in.

My sister—she bellowed some more insults. Ridiculous ones. I shook them off the way a dog shakes off water after a swim in the sea.

I realized it all so clearly then: I created the Natascha I needed—a counterpart to evil, an alibi for myself, a reassurance that there was someone lovable in my family and therefore, some semblance of normality to our lives, so that we were not all bad stock.

But today—now—none of that matters anymore.

I watched her go—a thin woman carrying a rucksack . . . and a soul full of spite.

Yes, I hurt. The pain washed over me in big, heavy waves. But strangely, I felt all the stronger for it. It felt like those same waves lifted a heavy burden off of me and washed it away.

I didn't lose a sister.

I lost an illusion.

And regained myself, once and for all.

THE END

SISTERLY SCORN
Will I ever be forgiven?

I didn't want to look, but I had to face reality. How many months had it been? Three? Four? I had let time slip by without bothering to keep track. I took a deep breath, splashed water on my face, and squinted at the pregnancy test. There was a stupid little plus sign in a stupid little window. I let out my breath.

Whom am I calling stupid? I switched my gaze from the plus sign to the man snoring in the bed. He was a definite minus. How did I get hooked up with a con-artist like Joey? Okay, so he said he liked my style, and he was kind of cute. And I told myself that Joey was better than a pimp was. I was only pulling cons, not tricks. At least, that's how I justified it.

My hands were still wet, and I shoved them through my hair. I looked in the mirror. The bruise on my cheek was turning purple, and I probed the split on my lip with my tongue. This was one of Joey's more modest efforts.

I closed my eyes, wondering if it would still be all right to pray. It had been a long time since I'd prayed—I couldn't remember when—and now I was pregnant. I needed help.

I hauled a duffel bag out of the closet and began to pack my stuff, not that there was much. Two-bit scams pay the rent and put food on the table, but that's about it. Jeans and T-shirts were as good as we got. I did have one nice dress, just in case we needed it for a big con—not that we ever pulled a big con.

Well, one good dress would have to be enough to get me a job interview. I hated to do it, but I was going to crawl back to Daddy. All I wanted was a job, and my computer skills were still good. I figured I could be happy in data processing.

I didn't have any reason to think Daddy would take me back, since I'd used my considerable computing skills to hack into my trust account. I cleaned it out and split. I wasn't ever going to go back home, at least, that's what I thought back then.

I hated the label of being "Daddy's girl." It made me feel like I was being smothered with someone else's identity. I wanted to be my own girl. I took the money and ran. By the way, let me emphasize that it was my money, and Daddy let me go. He never pressed charges.

Just a job, please, Daddy? You don't even have to look at me. I'll work down on the seventh floor. I'll get an apartment on the other side of town. I'll even look different. I hope the people in personnel don't remember that my name is Vincenza. Then they won't tell Daddy that I'm here. I just want a job.

Was that a prayer? That's what I was thinking as I threw my clothes into the bag.

Joey snorted and turned over. I checked, but he was still asleep. Not surprising, he had been out the night before and came home plastered. I guess, I got in his way when he tried to find the bed. Result? One bruised cheek.

What had I seen in that jerk? I must have been a sucker for a guy who'll pick you off the streets. Thank goodness, it never occurred to me to marry him. I kissed him good-bye, picked up the duffel bag, and closed the door behind me.

I had just enough money for a one-way bus ticket. The bus got me in town shortly after noon. I had plenty of time to change clothes at the bus station and put on some makeup before the personnel office closed. I noticed with annoyance that my nice dress was unfashionably snug—the baby was already making its presence known.

The bruise didn't look too bad with foundation on it, and my sunglasses hid the worst. I didn't know what to do with the duffel bag. There were lockers at the bus station, but it was too far from Daddy's office to walk back to retrieve it. So I lugged it with me. Maybe I could stuff it under a chair so it wouldn't be noticed.

I filled out a job application using the name Vincenza Western, and took a seat on one of the molded plastic chairs. Daddy had cushioned leather chairs in his own office, but this plastic one was better than the cracked wooden one I'd left behind. I was waiting, trying to think of the best way to explain three years with no employment records when Daddy burst in. I hadn't counted on the personnel manager spotting my social security number and reporting it to him.

"Vincenza!"

Then he swept me in his arms without a word. I knew I was trembling, but it felt so good to be held like that.

"It's wonderful to see you again," he said.

Daddy slid off my sunglasses and held my face between his hands. He didn't say a word about the bruise, but his thumb traced a scar near my eye. Another souvenir from Joey!

"Come on, Vincenza, we're going home."

"No," I protested. "Daddy, I just want a job. I can't come home with you."

"You're my daughter, of course you can."

"You don't understand—" I tried to explain, but he put his finger on my lips.

"Not another word. I've already called for the car. We're going home."

44

What could I say? I smeared away the tears with the back of my hand, dragged the duffel bag out from under the chair, and went home with Daddy.

He called for our housekeeper as soon as he opened the door. "Look who's home, Mrs. Handschu."

She clucked over me happily and snatched the duffel bag out of my hand. "I'll fix something special for dinner. Don't worry, I remember what Miss Vincenza likes."

I heard her chattering about grilled salmon and strawberry shortcake as she trotted down the hall. I hadn't had enough money to buy lunch, and my stomach growled in appreciation.

I followed Daddy into the living room. It seemed to me that the paintings, carpet, and furniture all had a special glow in the afternoon sun. I sank gratefully into a familiar chair. The room hadn't changed a bit and neither had Daddy. He looked just the same—well-cut suit, a splash of color in his silk tie, and graying hair combed back from his forehead.

He seemed happy just to sit and look at me. I started to tell him where I had been, but he just put a finger to his lips.

"It doesn't matter what happened these past three years, Vincenza. What matters is that you're back."

I hadn't counted on him being so nice. But I certainly hadn't counted on my sister, Marlena, being so angry. She must have noticed the flowers and other festive touches.

"What's going on?" We had no trouble hearing her shout from the front hall.

Mrs. Handschu bubbled. "Your sister's come home . . ."

"Vincenza? I don't believe it."

". . . And we're having a special welcoming dinner."

"You've got to be kidding. She practically robs Daddy, and you get out the good china? If you think I'm eating with her, think again. Send my dinner to my room. And it better not be what you fixed for her! If she deserves something special, so do I."

She didn't join us for dinner. Daddy cast one sorrowful glance at the empty place, then lifted his glass in a toast to me. I knew I didn't deserve all the commotion. But if Daddy wanted to make a fuss, I wasn't going to stop him. It had been so long since anyone had treated me nicely. I smiled and lifted my own glass.

Marlena appeared after dinner. She planted herself in the middle of the living room. She'd put her hands firmly on her hips, let her eyes rake me over, and then yelled. I stopped listening after a while, but it was interesting to see muscle quivering along her clenched jaw.

"Look at her, Daddy." Actually, Marlena didn't need to say that, Daddy couldn't keep his eyes off me. "Who knows where she's been? Obviously, in a fight."

"It's been a long day," he said smoothly.

That was not enough to detour, Marlena. "You look like a tramp."

For some reason, that cracked my silence. "Oh, yeah? Well I'm not. I wouldn't have gotten myself knocked up by my boyfriend if I were, would I?"

I hadn't meant to blurt it out like that, but I'd never be able to keep that a secret.

My sister didn't miss a beat. "Pregnant! It figures. So what have you been doing? Hooking? Do you have a clue who the father is?"

"I may be a lot of nasty things in your book, sis, but I'm not a whore. I already told you it was my boyfriend, and his name is Joey. I lived with him—and only him—for almost a year."

"And just what kind of man is this Joey?"

"He happens to be a—an artist."

Okay, Joey is a two-bit crook, I admit it, but it sounded much worse coming from Marlena, so I just left out the "con" part and went with "artist." I didn't have much face left, but I wanted to save something.

Daddy hadn't said much so far, but now he stood up and took my hand. "Come on, Vincenza. It's time for bed." He strode down the hall with me to my old bedroom.

Nothing he had said or done so far spoke to me the way that old room did. It was just how I had left it. I ran my hand over the top of my computer. I thought he'd have gotten rid of that for sure, but it sat on the desk where I had used it to plan my escape. It was strange, somehow, but this room felt like home now. It wasn't the prison I used to think it was.

Or maybe I had just figured out who I was.

"Daddy, I don't know what to say."

"Don't say anything, Vincenza. We'll talk about the baby later."

"I'm not getting an abortion."

"Of course not." He smiled. "Get some rest now. You're going to need it." He turned at the door, adding, "Welcome home."

Daddy gave me my old job back, which meant, of course, that I would have to work in the same department as Marlena. I told him I didn't think that was a good idea.

"Can't I just have a job in data processing?"

"Don't be silly, Vincenza. You were one of the best in the computer department. Don't you think you can handle the work anymore?"

"I can handle the work, but won't it be embarrassing for you? I mean, I'm obviously single, and, pretty soon, it will be obvious that I'm pregnant."

"Are you embarrassed?" Daddy looked me squarely in the

eye. "If you are, I suppose you could always hide behind 'Vincenza Western.'"

I sighed. "I'm not planning to hide anymore, Daddy."

"Okay. You start day after tomorrow. First get yourself some new clothes."

My sister did not let this go without making her position clear. "Daddy, this isn't fair. She's been gone all this time, and now you buy her new clothes and give her back her old job? You're even giving her the same pay as me! Don't try to deny it; I checked with personnel." She strode toward the door, then turned. "How do you think I feel? After all these years, it's like a slap in the face."

"It's not a slap, Marlena. She was good at that job, and I hire good people."

"What about me? Aren't I good?"

It was too bad for that Marlena made her exit then. She didn't hear Daddy say: "You're better than good, Princess; you're the best."

I dreaded my first day on the job. I thought I would be feeling the acid side of my sister's tongue all day, but she barely said a word. It took three weeks before the rumors that she was spreading came back around to my office. I didn't know which I hated more: the whispers or those quick, furtive looks.

Marlena seemed amazed that I had gone through all that money in three years so I decided to set her straight. I confess I wanted to present my case with the maximum amount of shock value. I noticed quite a few people from our department in the lunchroom that day as I began my story.

"Actually, dear sister, I got through the money in two years. Last year I lived with Joey, remember?"

She rolled her eyes. "I can't imagine how you could go through that much cash. What did you do? Drugs?"

"So tell me, sis, have you ever tried a line of coke?" Drugs hadn't been there at the beginning, only at the end. "You want to know what I did with the money, Marlena? I had fun. F-U-N. I bet you don't even know what the word means."

"I'm sure your kind of 'fun' is hardly what I would consider fun."

I made myself comfortable on the table. "You might have thought some of the things I did were fun. I bought clothes, jewelry, a pricey car, and lots of friends. I went to shows and took a cruise. Doesn't champagne on the beach sound like fun?" Should I tell her the drinking led to gambling? "Then I came home and went to the local gambling casinos. I only started to use drugs when the money started to disappear."

Did drugs. Wasn't that a cute way to say it? I didn't want to admit

47

I had been addicted. I didn't want to talk about that last party that landed me in the hospital. I had awakened with no money, no place to go, and no more ritzy friends. Joey looked pretty good to me then.

Marlena winked at a friend. "What happened then?"

"I—uh—had an accident and ended up in the hospital. I met Joey when I got out. I didn't have a place to go, so he took me home with him."

"How gallant of him. Then what? Did you just desert him?"

It was hard to stay composed when I could practically taste her sneers. "I left him because he used to beat me up. I was afraid he would kill our baby."

That statement had plenty of shock value. Marlena was silent, but someone human said, "Vincenza, how awful. Why did you stay with him?"

I was close to tears. "Joey said he loved me, and I thought I loved him, too. I probably would have been arrested for shoplifting, if he hadn't taken me in. Joey taught me a few things about the world that good girls like you will never know. I owe him. And—I'm not sorry he got me pregnant."

The other girls were gaping and my composure suddenly shattered. I ran for the ladies' room. After I lost my breakfast, I took a good look in the mirror. The strange thing was, I liked what I saw—Daddy's girl. But this wasn't the "daddy's girl" trapped in a corporate box.

I had changed. There was the scar and the other little bruises. I turned sideways, admiring how the well-cut maternity outfit flattered my blossoming figure. I had come to terms with the consequences of what I had done, and, somehow, took joy in carrying Joey's baby. I smiled at my reflection and squared my shoulders. Then I went back to work.

Although Marlena stopped talking to me, things went smoothly at work. I easily fell back into the old routine. I found satisfaction in doing the job well, and I was much better at this than anything I had done on the street. I made friends with the people I worked with who hadn't joined Marlena's silent faction. The past was truly over, and I could see new possibilities opening before me. Only the kicking baby connected me to Joey now.

Daddy came to me one day with a proposal. There was an opening in the other office, and he wanted to know if I was interested.

"Doesn't this mean a promotion, Daddy?"

He grinned. "Of course."

"Shouldn't Marlena have had first refusal?"

"Well, you can both do the job, but I've sensed friction between you two."

"Hmm. Friction implies heat; this is more like a cold war." I sighed. Not redeveloping a sisterly relationship was my one regret at returning home. "I've tried, Daddy. She won't talk to me."

"I know. And don't think I don't realize that she's recruited half the office. I thought you might like to start fresh. You won't run into her prejudices in the other office."

"I'm not running anymore. Offer her the job; she deserves the promotion, as well as the chance to put some space between us."

"Is that what you want?"

"Yes, Daddy."

"No matter what, I love both my daughters. No matter what."

"I know that." I threw my arms around him and got a bear hug in return. "Daddy, I love you, too."

Months passed, and it was time for our annual company dinner. I looked forward to the elegant evening, counting down the last few days of pregnancy and hoping the baby's appearance would hold off until afterward.

Daddy came to my door that evening as I finished dressing. He held out a jewelry box. "These belonged to your mother. I thought they would look pretty on you."

I opened the box. The earrings were large amethysts circled by pearls, the glowing purple exactly matching my gown. Standing in front of the mirror, I clipped them on. "Thank-you, Daddy. They're perfect."

Marlena paused in the doorway. "I liked it better when you looked like a tramp."

"Thank-you, Marlena. You look nice, too."

Daddy interrupted this face-off. "What is the matter with you girls?"

"After what she did to you," Marlena jabbed a finger at me, "how can you take her back, give her jewels, even show her off in public in her condition?"

"She looks beautiful. And it doesn't matter what she did; she's my daughter, just as you are. I love her. I forgive her."

I sighed. "I did do some things I'm not proud of, Marlena. I wish I could wipe everything clean from my past, but I can't. Some of the consequences will be with me forever, like this one." I patted my bulging belly. "But I didn't hurt you. Can't we start over?"

"I don't see how Daddy can forgive you." She snorted. "I never will."

"Fair enough. Do you know what forgiveness means? It means you don't ask for compensation. So, if you can't forgive, I have to pay back. What do you want from me?"

She crossed her arms. "You couldn't possibly have anything I

49

want. And you don't deserve anything at all—except punishment."

I sighed. "You're right; I should be punished. And I have been. That's one reason I stayed with Joey—I thought I deserved to be beaten. And no, I don't deserve this house, these earrings, a new start—but I didn't ask for them, either. All I asked from Daddy was a job. It was a miracle he gave me forgiveness as well."

"I never want to see you again," she spat.

"I guess that could happen. I know Daddy offered you the job in the other office. If you take it, you won't have to lay eyes on me. Is that what you want?"

She glared at me. "I hate you."

Tears pricked my eyes. "I could live with that, but I'd rather have a sister."

"You got it all, didn't you?"

"Yeah, Marlena, you're right. I took it all. Then I found out what happens when you lose it all. Don't forget there was a time when I had nothing, when I might have landed in jail."

"I may have it all now, but you've always had it. Don't you realize that?"

Marlena scowled at the floor, but I saw her shoulders begin to unclench. Please, God let her thaw. I held out my hand, hoping for my sister's touch.

I knew that I hadn't deserved her forgiveness or friendship, but I was hoping to get it one day.

"You're my sister, so I'll have to forgive you eventually. But I'm still angry with you," she said.

"Oh, Marlena, thank-you. You're going to be a wonderful aunt!"

"I don't think I'll take the promotion. Someone has to help you raise that baby. And who knows what kind of mother you'll be. That baby is going to need with a levelheaded aunt."

I smiled. Marlena and I still had a long way to go, but we were on the right track.

THE END

IF HE DIES . . .

"Mama sad," Kennedy announced from the highchair when her daddy came home in from work. "She cry."

"Honey, what's wrong?" John asked, his voice filled with concern as he tried to encircle me in his arms. Try was about all he could do. I was seven months pregnant and big as a house.

"Nothing," I stammered. "I'm all right."

"Brenda, you're not all right. Is it the baby? You're not in labor, are you?"

"No," I choked in reply. Just having his arms around me made me feel better.

"Daddy! Daddy! Do I look pretty?" our older daughter asked as she twirled around the small kitchen. "I got lots of new dresses from Stephanie. Look at how this one sparkles!"

"Yes, darling, you look like a princess," he answered off-handedly as Brooke ran back to her room to try on another outfit.

"Brenda," John began again, quickly turning his attention back to me. "What's wrong?"

"That's what's wrong." I sobbed, pointing to Brooke. "She's been trying on those beautiful clothes ever since Minnie left."

"Honey, I don't understand. You're upset because Brooke is trying on some new dresses?"

"But they're not new," I replied impatiently. "They're Stephanie's hand-me-downs. I don't want my daughter to have to wear her cousin's old clothes."

"Your stepsister always gives Brooke the clothes Stephanie outgrows. Sylvia loves to shop. And you know she can afford to buy the best. I bet half of those dresses were only worn once or twice."

"That's the same thing Minnie said." I pouted, tears rolling down my face.

"Mama cry when Nana go bye bye," Kennedy contributed to the conversation.

John went over and lifted the baby out of her highchair. "Maybe you can tell me what happened here today," he asked our two-and-a-half-year-old daughter after he kissed her chubby pink cheeks.

Brooke continued her fashion show, this time wearing a full-length coat.

"Feel how soft this is Mama," she exclaimed, gently guiding my hand over the luxurious material.

"Brooke, honey, tell me what happened today," John inquired, trying to make some sense of what was going on.

"Grandma Minnie brought me lots of pretty clothes and she told Mama not to have any more babies and not to buy a . . . I think a trail house, then she left, and Mama's been crying ever since," Brooke recounted the afternoon's events quite accurately.

John scooted the girls into the living room and put one of their tapes in the VCR.

"A trail house? What's that all about? And Minnie told you not to have any more babies?" John asked, pulling me into his arms again.

I nodded sadly.

"I mentioned to Minnie that we asked Sylvia to look for a piece of property for us to put a preconstructed home on. She had the nerve to say if we're going to put a trailer on a lot in this county, we better check with the neighbors to see if they approve! I informed her that a preconstructed home isn't a trailer. It took all I had not to break down in front of her. I'm depressed enough being pregnant again without my stepmother making me feel like—"

"Sweetheart, don't cry," he soothed, tenderly rubbing the small of my back. "Those preconstructed homes we toured were very nice and they cost a lot less than building a new house. I don't understand how you could be friends with your stepsister and barely tolerate her mother."

"Because Sylvia is a nice person and Minnie. . . . Minnie was bragging about how successful Sylvia is at selling real estate. She sold three houses her first month on the job. Her commission was over fifteen thousand dollars. It takes us months to make that much money. And Minnie knew I was planning to work a full-time job when I got pregnant again. She knows how rough things have been for us."

"I understand why you're so blue, hon. But it will get better. You know I help you as much as I can."

I didn't even bother to tell John how much I appreciated all he did. "This haircut is terrible. I'm fat and depressed. I feel like I've been pregnant for a year." I moaned, stomping my foot loudly on the floor, as if that was going to change anything.

"Well you know what I told you, sugar. If it's a boy this time, then you can quit having babies," John replied, his eyes twinkling as he teased a smile out of me.

"Oh I'm quitting." I laughed. "Boy, girl, or whatever. This is definitely our last child!"

"Mama, I'm hungry. What's for dinner?" Brooke called out from the living room.

"Hungee. Me hungee, too," Kennedy echoed.

"Dinner. I didn't even start—"

John held his hand up in a motion for me to stop talking. "I was reading meters in my mom's neighborhood today. She had a pot of spaghetti sauce on the stove, so naturally I wrangled an invitation for dinner. I'll take a quick shower and we can leave."

"But we had dinner there twice this week."

"She insisted," John replied, heading toward the bathroom.

"You don't have to twist my arm," I answered, relieved that I didn't have to cook. I loved John's mom and she was a wonderful mother-in-law. We'd become good friends since John and I were married six years ago.

Brooke and Kennedy came running into the kitchen.

"We're going to Grandma Dottie's." Brooke clapped in delight.

"Gamma Dede." Kennedy clapped in unison. "Mama happy?"

"Yes, sweetie pie, Mama's happy," I answered, handing my precious daughters each a cookie. "This will hold you over until dinner."

"Cookies are like kisses. One's never enough!" Brooke giggled as she held her hand out for another. "Isn't that what you always say?"

"One 'nuff?" Kennedy mimicked, stretching her chubby hand out.

"Okay," I relented, as I always did. "Two, but no more. We'll be eating dinner soon."

Brooke and Kennedy dashed back into the living room to finish watching their tape. I reached for a cookie, remembering all the times my mother told me cookies were like kisses . . . that seemed to be one of the only things I remember clearly. The cookie jar was always full.

I was only seven when my mother died, but recently I've been thinking about her a lot. Maybe it's because I'm having my third child and I was the third one in our family. I remember waiting for Mom to come home with the pizza that was going to be our dinner. But she never came home again. In a few moments my life was turned upside down. My mother was dead, and deep inside I knew it was my fault.

"Ready, darling?"

"Huh? Oh, yeah," I answered, clearing the cobwebs from my mind. "I'm ready."

After dinner, John and his dad took the girls outside to play while Dottie and I did the dishes. More accurately, Dottie cleared the table while I drank lemonade.

"I didn't feel like this when I was pregnant before. I'm starting to worry that something might be wrong," I confided.

"Honey, it's those hormones swimming around your system. I had five kids. I know what you're going through. Believe me, once the baby's here you'll be your old self again," Dottie assured me.

"John thinks it's a boy this time."

"Or it could be twins. They do run on my side of the family."

"Don't remind me about that! I'm getting another ultrasound tomorrow. Maybe the doctor will tell me I'm going early," I stated wistfully.

"I'll be over in plenty of time for you to get ready."

"Thanks, Dottie. I don't know what I'd do without you. I better round up the troops. Thanks for everything," I said, as I gave my mother-in-law a big hug of appreciation.

My obstetrician's examination was longer than usual the next day. He told the technician to call him into the room when she started the ultrasound. A wave of panic started forming deep inside me.

"Dr. Alton, is my baby okay? What's wrong?" I pleaded, sure the doctor knew something was amiss. Guilt washed over me. All the complaining I do . . . I don't mean it . . . all I want is a healthy baby.

"Relax, Mrs. Coleman. Everything looks great," he finally assured me. "Do you want to be surprised this time or would you like to know the sex?"

"I want to know what it is," I whispered with a sigh of relief once my doctor confirmed that the baby was normal.

"It's a boy."

"That's wonderful. John will be thrilled. I guess he was right. Having a boy is different than being pregnant with a girl."

"That might account for a slight difference," Dr. Alton continued as he helped me to a sitting position. "But I suspect it's really due to the fact that you're having twins!"

"You're joking," I said in disbelief, yet knowing by the look on his face that he wasn't.

"Two boys. The second one must've been hiding behind his brother all this time. That's why we didn't see him when we did the first ultrasound. This changes things for you considerably. I want you to rest as much as possible. I'll examine you every week. In addition, you'll have to come into the office three times a week, Monday, Wednesday, and Friday to be hooked up to the cardiac monitor. It's important that we watch the babies closely. And unless that boy in the back turns down, which I doubt, we'll have to do C-section. I know it's easy for me to say not to worry, but I've delivered many sets of twins, so trust me, everything will work out fine," he reassured me. "And congratulations!"

I don't know how I drove home. I was in a daze. It felt like a cruel joke was being played on me. All right, Brenda Coleman, you want to complain about having another baby? How would you like to have two babies?

"What's wrong?" Dottie asked when I walked slowly into the kitchen. "You're white as a sheet."

I opened my mouth to explain, but nothing came out. For the first time in my life I was literally speechless.

"Brenda, is the baby okay? What is it?"

"Twins," I finally managed to squeak out when I found my voice. "Twins." Then I covered my face with my hands and sobbed.

"Twins! Why that's wonderful, honey! Is the doctor sure? Why didn't he let you know sooner? And where are you going to put two babies?" Dottie asked in a rush.

I'd asked myself those same questions a hundred times driving home. I repeated to Dottie what the doctor had told me. Brooke and Kennedy had grasped enough to understand that they were going to be having two new babies instead of just one.

Dottie insisted on taking the girls home with her so I could rest. When John came home and I broke the news to him, he reacted as if we'd won the lottery. The more I thought about it—and having two babies was the only thing on my mind right now—I realized how expensive it was going to be to raise twins. I couldn't pass dresses or pink play suits down to little boys, and besides, I'd need double of everything.

Our house only had two bedrooms. We were trying to save for a bigger house, but when you're raising two kids there isn't very much extra money to put in the bank each month.

I'd planned on adding several new accounts to the medical transcription business I worked from my home computer, but now I didn't think I'd even be able to handle the two doctors who were using my service.

The only solution I could come up with was for John to get another job. He didn't mind working a second job, but he wanted to wait until after the babies were born. I convinced him to find something as soon as possible. I thought that would be best. I was only thinking of our family.

"It's going to be awfully hard for you to manage the girls without my help," John pointed out. "It's not going to be easy for either of us."

"If I had to chose between a second job or taking care of four kids under six, with three in diapers. . . ." I couldn't even finish the sentence. Tears were flowing again.

"I guess both boys can sleep in one crib for a little while," I continued when I pulled myself together again. "Then we'll have to put a crib in the living room. I can just hear what Minnie will have to say about that!"

"Forget about her. You go finish your nap. I'll go get the girls from my mom's and bring a bucket of chicken home for dinner. Now off to bed with you!" he commanded with mock sternness and a gentle pat on my ample behind.

"That's what got me into this predicament," I mumbled as I headed toward the bedroom.

A few days later John started working at a sporting goods store. They were willing to schedule him a few evenings a week and on his days off. The pay was decent and he could earn a commission if his sales were high enough.

Although we were desperately going to need a bigger house, it took me all of about three days to realize I'd made a big mistake in forcing John to take this second job now.

Normally he came home from the water company at three thirty and he would help me with dinner and getting the girls bathed and to bed. Now he dashed in, showered, grabbed a sandwich, and was out the door by four to get to his night job by four thirty.

I should've told him how difficult it was becoming for me to function without him home in the evenings and asked him to quit, but then he got his first paycheck. It was almost as much as the salary from his day job. He was so proud of his big commission check, and how quickly we'd be able to have the down payment for a bigger house. I didn't have it in me to burst his bubble.

I didn't have much longer to go. Dottie came over every day and Sylvia usually stopped by on her way home from work to check on me. I'll be able to manage, I told myself over and over. My doctor says another week. Ten days at the most.

I didn't think anything could happen to make my life more difficult than it already was right now, but it did.

Dottie's mom fell and sprained her ankle. Dottie wanted to bring her to her house to recuperate, but my father-in-law is allergic to cats and Grandma Arthur had three of them. Dottie would be at her mom's in Springfield for at least a week. Maybe two!

The babies were getting big, and my obstetrician didn't want to risk my health waiting for the original due date. He informed me that Friday that if my labor didn't start by the end of next week, I'd go into the hospital and have the babies by Cesarean section.

That's what prompted John to call and ask my sister for help. I was so desperate I didn't object when John told me what he'd done. To my surprise, Dana agreed to come down the next day.

"I didn't know what else to do, babe, but with my mom out of town and Sylvia working full time . . . well, Dana didn't seem to mind at all. I probably should've asked you before I called, but. . . ."

"You're very considerate, John, but I don't know. I mean, I'm surprised Dana agreed to it."

"She didn't even know you having twins. When was the last time you talked to her?"

"A couple months ago," I answered quietly. "Maybe it wasn't such a good idea. We're not very close like sisters should be."

"It's all arranged, babe. I can't concentrate on either job worrying about you all the time," John retorted, glancing at his watch. "I got to go, darling. I'll call you during my break. Dana said she'd be here by five. Bye. Love you."

A quick kiss on the cheek and he was gone again.

"Love you, too," I waved as John bounded out the door.

Brooke and Kennedy were playing quietly together in their room, so I was able to sit down and relax for a bit.

The words I'd said to John a few moments ago were dancing in my head. We're not very close like sisters should be. . . .

Dana was sixteen years older than me. There was a brother between us, but Phil lived on the west coast and hadn't been back to Charleston in years. My sister lived about thirty miles away but we rarely saw one another. She came to Dad's around Christmas and that was the only time I'd see her. Once a year. No phone calls, no visiting each other. We weren't close at all.

I was seven when our mom died. Dana was twenty-three, married with a little boy. Our brother, Phil, was away at college. Neither of them seemed to be as devastated as I was by our mother's death. I was only a child, but I sensed they didn't care that she died.

Dana lived nearby then, and would come home several times a week. I'd go to her house after school, and Dad and I went there for Sunday dinner. Then dad married Minnie and Dana's visits home became less frequent.

My stepsister, Sylvia, was two years older than me and we got along great. After a while, I realized Minnie treated her daughter better than me. But I didn't hold it against Sylvia. She was a nice, honest person, not phony and pretentious like her mother. My stepmother seemed to take pleasure in hurting my feelings and making me feel inferior to her daughter.

Minnie succeeded in driving a wedge between me and my dad. I didn't see him too often. Our family wasn't very close-knit. I planned on raising my children to love and get along with their siblings. My family was going to be different.

"Mama. Mama. Somebody's knocking. Wake up." Brooke was shaking my arm. "Wake up."

"Oh . . . I dozed off. Okay, baby, I'll get the door," I replied, slowly easing myself out of the recliner to answer the front door.

"Dana. Hi. Hope you weren't waiting too long. I sat down and must've fallen asleep for a few minutes. Come in."

"Brenda," Dana exclaimed happily, putting her arms around me in a warm greeting. "You look wonderful. I can't believe you're going to have twins. And your hair looks great," she remarked, gently running her fingers through my strands. "We have the same hairdo and practically the same figure!"

"Dana, you look fine. It's nice to see you. Come on in."

"Who is this?" Brooke whispered, half-hiding behind me.

"It's your Aunt Dana, honey. Mama's sister," I explained. "Do you remember seeing her at Grandpa Bob's on Christmas Eve?"

"She looks like you," Brooke observed with a smile.

"We look more alike than you want to admit," Dana chuckled unselfconsciously. "I gave up trying to lose weight six months ago when I turned forty. I bought every diet book ever written and none do any good. I'm fat and that's that! If anyone doesn't like it, well, it's their problem, not mine."

"You look healthy. That's what John tells me. Come on in, sit down. It was so kind of you to come and help me out. Did you have dinner? How about a cup of coffee or an iced tea?"

"You sit yourself down, Mama. Your big sister is in charge now," she commanded cheerfully. "I'll bring my things from the car. Then I'll eat and have a nice visit."

Dana brought dinner and a homemade chocolate cake. Brooke and Kennedy were immediately enthralled with their vivacious aunt. She'd steal kisses and playfully tweak their cheeks, much to their delight. They put up a big fuss at bedtime but finally gave in when I assured them that Aunt Dana would still be here in the morning.

For the past few weeks the only place I could even halfway comfortably sleep was in the worn out leather recliner in the living room. Fortunately our sofa opened into a bed, but Dana didn't want to make it up until after John came home. She was so sweet with the girls and considerate to me. I was overwhelmed by her kindness.

"Dana, I can't tell you how much I appreciate you coming here to help me. It won't be long. My doctor thinks I'll have the baby, I mean babies, within a week or so."

"Since Brad's death and with Sam away at college, my time is my own. I'll stay with you as long as you need me."

"I have to admit I was a little apprehensive when John told me he called you."

"Why on earth would you feel apprehensive about asking me for help?" Dana interrupted.

"I didn't know if you'd want to, or, I don't know, maybe it's because I'm pregnant and all the hormones and stuff, but I've been thinking an awful lot about our mother and our family, and . . ." I hesitated before saying it, hoping I wouldn't offend her, "I mean, do you ever wonder why we weren't close? I mean like other sisters?"

Dana sat silently for a few moments, looking as if she was choosing her words very carefully before speaking.

"The easy answer would be the difference in our ages, and I guess when we were young that was true but now—" Dana began then abruptly stopped talking for a few seconds. "Honey, I know what you mean about being pregnant, how it can cause so many changes, so maybe this isn't the best time to go tromping down memory lane. Sometimes reminiscing isn't all fun. It can be painful, too."

"I have been pretty emotional," I admitted with a wry smile.

"You emotional?" John snickered, hearing the end of our conversation as he walked into the living room.

"Don't say another word, mister! Not if you want your dinner, and I'll tell you right now, my sister is a terrific cook. Wait until you taste the Beef Stroganoff she brought."

"I'll get it," Dana offered, giving John a hug. "And thanks for calling me. I'm so glad to help my little sister."

"Little sister?" John repeated in an exaggerated whisper.

"Don't go there, John." I laughed, wagging my finger in a playful warning.

Laughing was something I hadn't been doing too much of lately, but spending a few hours with my sister made me feel calm and relaxed.

I think Brooke and Kennedy enjoyed their Aunt Dana's visit as much as I did. The last month or two hadn't been too easy on them. We used to go to the game farm, the duck pond, or the aviary at least once a week. We were regulars at our library's preschool story hour and often visited friends of mine who also had young children, but recently I was too tired for any social activities.

Dana colored with Brooke and Kennedy, took them for walks, and even put on a puppet show with puppets she and the girls made from a bag of socks I was going to throw away.

Happily, the next few days went by smoothly. The weather was turning warm and I thought it would be nice to have a cookout that afternoon before John went to work. He cleaned the gas grill but when he tried to light it, the ignition valve had rusted and couldn't get it to fire. He insisted on rummaging through the basement for the old charcoal grill and in the process cut his arm on a pair of hedge clippers. I thought he was going to need stitches to stop the bleeding, but Dana iced the wound and bandaged him up.

Then the manager of the store called and asked John to come in early. One man called off sick and they were swamped with customers because of the nice weather. John started to refuse, but I urged him to go because by that time, it was too late to cook out and have time to eat. John made himself a sandwich, grumbling about not having the time to eat a decent meal anymore, and walked out the door.

Next Brooke and Kennedy got into a struggle over a toy and before I could get them apart, Brooke was on the ground with a bump rising up on her forehead from colliding into the fence. After that

59

medical emergency was taken care of, Dana offered to take the girls to the park so I could rest. I was only too happy to comply with her suggestion. I settled into the recliner and quickly fell into a light sleep when I heard knocking on the door. My stepmother dropped by. Just what I needed to make the day worse than it already was.

"I think these lots might be out of your price range," Minnie remarked as she handed me the listings Sylvia had prepared. "I know you need more room but—"

"John and I know what we can afford," I shot back haughtily.

"I didn't mean to imply . . . look at you! I don't know how you can move. You're huge!" Minnie exclaimed when I finally heaved myself out of the recliner. "I swear, you must've gained twenty pounds since the last time I saw you."

"I'm ready to deliver twins! What do you expect me to look like? A fashion model?" I practically shouted at her, not even trying to keep the contempt out of my voice. "If you came here to insult me, you've done it, now why don't you leave?"

"Brenda. I'm sorry. I didn't mean . . . I was only. . . ."

"I don't care what you meant. I'm tired of you looking down on me and my family. Bragging all the time about how successful Sylvia is. Giving Brooke Sofia's hand-me-downs. Acting like John doesn't provide for us like he should. Telling me I look like a whale. . . ."

"Brenda, I never said such a thing."

"Maybe you never came right out and said it, but I know what you're implying and I'm tired of it."

"What's going on here?" Dana asked when she walked in during my confrontation with Minnie.

"Nothing. I'm leaving," Minnie replied and headed out the door.

"If you can't be a little more considerate toward my sister maybe you better not come here. You certainly have a knack for upsetting her," Dana whispered harshly to our stepmother.

Minnie didn't reply except for a huffing noise as she walked out the door.

"Are you okay, sweetie?" Dana asked, handing me a paper towel to wipe my eyes with. "I'm glad the girls stayed out in the yard and didn't see this scene. What's with that woman?"

"She's mean, spiteful, and thinks she's better than everybody else. How much money you make is the most important thing. Well, we're going to have a nice house and good furniture one of these days," I raved on.

Dana looked at me with surprise written on her face. "I always thought you liked Minnie."

"I did, until I got to know what she's really like, but I don't want to talk about her. I have to sit down." I sighed heavily. "My back is aching."

Brooke and Kennedy, who usually played fine together, were being downright nasty to each other that day. The ache in my back was getting worse. The casserole Dana made for dinner ran over the pan and created a big, burnt mess in the oven, setting off the smoke detector. It was an all around bad day but the worst was yet to come. Far worse.

Dana gave the girls their bath earlier than usual, hoping to quiet them down, but it had the opposite effect. Brooke got soap in her eyes which set off a screaming frenzy. Kennedy tried to take off before she was dried, then slipped and hurt her knee.

My daughters carried on for almost half an hour instead of going to sleep. When I couldn't take it anymore, Dana suggested putting Brooke in my bed until she fell asleep. One of the local stations was running a classic children's movie, so thankfully Brooke finally quieted down to watch it.

Dana fixed us a cup of peppermint tea and we shared the last few homemade cookies she'd brought over. The ache in my back wasn't letting up. I'd take a warm shower later, maybe it would help, but for now I just wanted to enjoy the peace and quiet for a few moments.

"Mama! Mama! Come look at the TV," Brooke shouted, as she ran into the living room.

"Baby, I'm too tired," I began, but then I noticed a look of fear on Brooke's sweet little face. "What's wrong?"

"I think the store where Daddy's working is on the news. I was watching the movie."

It felt like someone poured a bucket of ice water down my spine. My throat grew tight and dry and breathing seemed impossible for the next few seconds. My hands flew to my face as Dana turned on the TV in the living room. If I covered my eyes and didn't look at the screen . . . it couldn't be at the store John was working at.

"Oh dear God," I pleaded frantically. "Let my husband be safe!"

The words Breaking News rolled across the bottom of the TV.

"That's the store Daddy showed us on our way to . . ." Brooke said, her small voice trembling. "He told. . . ."

"Hush," I commanded instantly. "Yes, I think so. Maybe it's one of their other stores. . . ." I babbled fearfully. My heart was pounding fiercely. Seconds ago, I'd felt like I couldn't get any air into my body, now I was gulping as if oxygen was being dumped into my lungs by bucketfuls.

"Listen," I gulped, pointing to the somber-looking man on the screen.

Brooke began to whimper, sensing something was terribly wrong. Dana turned up the volume, then pulled Brooke close to her side and clutched my hand for support.

61

Over the next few moments, my worst fears were confirmed. The reporter read what little information they'd gotten from the police about the situation. A man had purchased a gun then became enraged when he found out he'd have to wait three days to pick it up. Another customer, who'd been in the store when the incident occurred, was on his cell phone in the parking lot when he recognized the man who'd caused the ruckus drive wildly to the front of the building, jump out of his car, and tear back into the store with a rifle in his hands.

He surmised what was about to happen and called 911. The police responded immediately, but they didn't know how many people were still in the store being held hostage by a crazed gunman!

Brooke understood enough to realize her daddy was in danger and she began crying harder. I started to tell Dana to call my neighbor when a great wave of pain overcame me. The horrific shock of learning my husband might be dead caused me to go into labor.

Dana called 911, realizing that it would be safer for the paramedics to transport me to the hospital. Then she went next door to get my neighbor to sit with the girls. The EMT arrived quickly.

Thankfully little Kennedy slept right through all the commotion. I hugged my older daughter tenderly, calling upon strength I didn't know I had to reassure her that her daddy would be fine.

Mrs. Adams was soothing Brooke with a story about how her baby brothers were going to be born, trying to take her mind off the tragedy that was unfolding in her family. I prayed that my daughter wouldn't have to endure the pain of losing a parent at such a young age, as I had.

At the hospital I was prepped for an immediate C-section. My doctor didn't want to risk a regular delivery after the shock I'd been through and the second boy was still in the breech position.

Dr. Alton assured me the delivery would go smoothly. Dana held my hand and wiped my forehead as my beautiful baby boys were born. This should've been the happiest day of my life but all I could think about was John. Was he still alive? Would he ever get to see his newborn sons?

Dr. Alton urged me to take a sedative to help me relax, but I refused. I had to stay awake until I knew John was all right. I must've been delirious or in a state of shock, but I felt that as long as I was awake, John would be safe.

Dana stayed by my side, watching over the babies, holding my hand, giving me her strength to get through this nightmare. I couldn't even find it in my heart to be happy about the two healthy baby boys I'd just delivered. I had to concentrate all my love and strength on John's well-being. I'd give my boys all the love and attention they deserved as soon as I knew their daddy was all right, and if he wasn't?

Would I be responsible for my husband's death like I was for my own mother's?

One hour dragged by, then two. Three turned into four. Fear and guilt were building up inside me, like a volcano ready to erupt. Dottie urged me to take some medication to ease the anxiety I was experiencing before I completely fell apart. I'd reacted badly to a sedative once before but I gave in when the doctor agreed to give me something mild, just to help me relax. But I didn't take it until we got word that the hostage situation had finally ended. After almost five agonizing hours the ordeal was over.

Two people were dead, three wounded. John was one of the fortunate ones. He'd been shot but the police informed me that the damage didn't appear to be life threatening. Dr. Alton came by to let me know that John was being readied for surgery and I'd be able to see him in a few hours.

Knowing that he was going to live made me relax a little. I was finally able to sleep for a short time with the help of the sedative. I remember seeing Dottie and Kennedy and my dad and Minnie, but I don't remember what they said or how long they were in my room.

When I woke up, the first light of dawn was edging across the horizon. Dana had fallen asleep in the chair. A tray of food was on the table across my bed. I opened the can of ginger ale to quench the awful tightness in my throat.

"You're awake?" Dana asked, shifting in her chair. "How are you feeling?"

Completely ignoring her question, I asked about John immediately. "Is he still in surgery? Is everything okay?"

"Surgery was completed a half hour ago. His doctor was here right before you woke up. John's in the recovery room and is doing fine, for all he'd been through. The next few hours are critical but he's optimistic that John will make a complete recovery. We're all praying for him, sweetie. His parents and his brothers and their families are here. So are Sylvia and her husband and Dad and Minnie. I know he's going to be all right."

Instead of being relieved that John was still alive, the information seemed to evoke more distress in me. My fear might have been irrational but it was very real to me.

"No. He's not going to make it." I sobbed. "Just like Mom. She made it through the surgery, but she died."

"Brenda, please. Don't do this to yourself. John's going to be fine. Do you want me to get his doctor so he can explain—"

"Dana, don't you see? It's happening again. It's my fault, just like when Mom died," I whispered.

It must have been a combination of the drugs they'd given me and the trauma of the past several hours that brought that awful day into sharp focus, forcing me to relive it once again.

"Why would you say that? You were a child. You were seven years old when Mom died. How on earth could you be responsible for her death?" Dana questioned me, dismay written on her face.

"It was my fault," I insisted. "I've felt that way all my life and I know that's why you didn't want to have anything to do with me. You blamed me, just like I blamed myself."

"What are you talking about? I never blamed you. Have you felt this way all these years? Please, Brenda, tell me what's going on. Please explain this to me," Dana asked, gently wiping the sweat that was forming on my forehead. "Tell me, honey. Get it off your chest."

I took a deep breath, trying to put into words the feelings that had been bottled up inside me for fourteen years. I'd never even told John.

"It was a Friday. Mom was going to make tuna casserole for dinner. That's what I had in school for lunch, so I asked for pizza. A new pizza shop had just opened down the road. Mom said she didn't know if Daddy would like pizza for dinner but I pleaded, not letting up until she finally agreed to go for it—"

"But that doesn't make you responsible for Mom's death." Dana interrupted.

"If I hadn't whined and insisted on having my own way, she'd still be alive today! And it's the same with John. He didn't want to get another job until after the babies were born, but I insisted. I had to have a bigger house. I complained about taking hand-me-down clothes for Brooke and Kennedy. I'm never satisfied with what I have until it's too late."

"Brenda, my heart's aching for you. To think that you carried this guilt all these years makes me so sad."

"But it was my fault," I repeated, tears falling down my face as I unburdened my life-long guilt.

"Brenda, think about it for a minute. Mom could've called and had the pizza delivered, couldn't she?"

"Delivered? I guess so. Yes, that's what Daddy said when he came home from work. He was very angry that I was alone," I answered, the memories slowly sifting back into my mind.

"Remember what I said the other day about how reminiscing can be painful? Honey, I hate to tell you this, but our mother was an alcoholic."

"What are you talking about?"

"You were too young to remember. Dad tried to get help for her, but she didn't want to quit. She didn't even have a driver's license. After the third drunk driving arrest—"

"But I wanted the pizza . . . she went there for me."

"There was a liquor store next to the pizza shop. That's why Mom went there. There was a case of vodka in the trunk of the car. One of the bottles was on the front seat when she crashed," Dana informed me, her voice straining with emotion. "You poor thing. All these years you blamed yourself."

"I thought that's why you didn't want anything to do with me. If you didn't blame me, why did you hardly ever come home?"

"It wasn't because of you, sweetheart. I guess I blamed Dad, but he'd tried to get her help. Maybe it was because of Minnie. I found out that he was having an affair with her while Mom was still alive. It really wasn't my place to judge them, but by then I was married and after Sam was born, I guess I felt like I didn't belong. And you seemed to be adjusting to your new life. I didn't want to remind you of the past."

"I didn't realize until this pregnancy how much I missed you," I declared, reaching up to give my sister a kiss. "I guess being pregnant can sure do some crazy things to your mind as well as your body."

"Whatever the reason, I'm thrilled it happened. You don't know how many times I wanted to visit you and see my nieces."

"Well all that's going to be different now," I replied, feeling myself smile for the first time. "John . . . do you think they'll let me see John? I want to see with my own eyes that he's still alive."

"I'll go talk to your nurse and see what I can do," Dana answered, kissing my cheek and hugging me before she left my bedside.

"It took some fast talking but they said I could take you to the recovery room, but you can only stay for a few minutes," she informed me when she came back.

"I just want to see him for myself," I repeated.

Dottie was standing beside the door of the unit. She reached out to me, tightly squeezing my hands in hers.

"The others went for coffee. The doctor just came by and checked John. He's responding wonderfully. I was going to come to your room soon."

A huge sigh of relief escaped from deep within me, and this time tears of joy flowed down my face.

"I was praying so hard. I knew he'd make it. Please, can I see him, just for a few moments?"

A nurse wheeled me to John's bedside. He was hooked up to tubes and monitors and enough machinery to build a small car. His color was a little pale but he didn't look nearly as bad as I expected he would.

I gently held his hand and whispered to him, even though I knew he couldn't hear me.

"John, darling. I'm so happy that you're alive. I'll never ask for

65

another thing in my life. We can live in a paper box, as long as I have you and the kids. I know there isn't anything more important than a loving family. Hurry and get well, so you can see those two beautiful little boys of ours. They need you and so do I."

A trace of a smile crossed John's face and he squeezed my hand gently. He'd heard me! He was going to make it!

"I love you, babe," he whispered slowly, opening his eyes for a few seconds. "I'll be fine."

Eventually he was. John had to go through several months of rehab then another operation on his leg. He was off work for a long time recuperating. But I'm convinced our kids—Brooke, Kennedy, Colin, and Curtis, had as much to do with his recovery as the doctors and medical professionals did.

And Dana. I don't know what I'd have done without my sister's help. She was a rock. She told me about things that went on in our family that I was too young to realize at the time. Like the cookie jar. Toward the end, Mom often forgot to go food shopping. So every time Dana came over, she'd bring a bag of cookies. That way she was sure I'd have something to eat. That's probably why a full cookie jar always seemed so important to me.

Now when I think back about how depressed I'd been when I got pregnant for the third time, I realize that if it hadn't happened, Dana might not have come back into my life.

Sylvia found a reasonably priced three-acre lot for us. We're going to put a preconstructed home on the far end this spring, and I think I've convinced Dana to put one on the other side of the property. She doesn't need her big house anymore and she wants to move closer to her family.

We have a lot of years to make up for, and Brooke and Kennedy have grown very fond of their Aunt Dana, as I'm sure Curtis and Colin will, too, when they get older.

My life couldn't be better. I have a wonderful, loving family, and there isn't anything more important than that.

THE END

HOLD ME, TOUCH ME
My sister begged my man

It had only been less than a year since I'd been home, but my Christmas visit brought with it an undeniable sense of reality that shook me to the very core. I may not have recognized my own mother had I seen her on the street. When I burst through the front door of my family home on Christmas Eve, I found her familiar eyes looking out at me from a weathered and tired face I scarcely knew. It took everything I had to hold back the tears of alarm that sprang up the moment I saw her.

She had mentioned the wheelchair once or twice in our weekly conversations, but I hadn't realized that she had become completely confined to it. Nor had I anticipated the slight curvature to the fingers of her left hand, or the mild whimper of pain that she uttered when I embraced her too enthusiastically.

My sister, Geralyn, still lived in the house with Mom, but it was really in name only. She'd stop by for an occasional shower or a place to crash between a night of partying and a morning shift at the local video store. And, what was worse, she didn't even seem to notice what had happened to our mother—right before her very eyes.

With those new revelations had come an eerie feeling, which had made that holiday a bittersweet one for me. While I was as happy to be home for a visit as I always was—Cold Harbor held much more charm for me when I was a temporary visitor than when I had been trapped there like a caged animal—I was overpowered by the ongoing and most unwelcome premonition that I was somehow going to be joining the ranks of the many escapees who eventually returned to our little town. I tried to attribute it to my own misgivings rather than to any real indication of future events, but that tiny quiver in my stomach continued to draw back my worst fears to the notion.

When the call had come from my mom's next-door neighbor, I hadn't really been surprised when she'd told me that Mom had taken a fall, lost consciousness, and that the doctors were keeping her overnight for observation.

"Perhaps you should think about a safer situation for her," Mrs. Walters commented. And, I knew that it had been distinctly more of a demand than the friendly suggestion that she'd tried to pretend it was. "Your mother isn't getting any younger," she pointed out as she continued. "Geralyn is gone for days on end, and living alone is a danger to her."

I knew that she was right, but the point had been driven cruelly home the moment I'd walked into the hospital room later that same day. Nothing on the long drive could have prepared me for what I found there, and I knew the moment that her frightened eyes met mine that nothing would ever be the same again.

Her face was badly bruised, and a bandage was wrapped awkwardly about her head where more than ten stitches had been necessary to repair the gash. The fear in her eyes melted into a strange sort of humiliation when she saw me, and her tears fell in sudden streams.

"Oh, honey, I'm sorry," she said immediately. She looked so small and frail in the stark, sterile room.

"Mom, you don't have to be sorry. I'm just so glad to see that you're all right," I told her.

But that was a lie. There was nothing about the sight of her lying there that made me feel even remotely relieved. Sheer panic bubbled up inside of me, and it took every ounce of strength I had to keep from crumpling into a hysterical mess in front of her.

"You didn't have to come all this way," she insisted. I thought of how ridiculous that sounded, but I didn't argue.

"Well, of course I did," I replied simply, then sat down on the edge of the bed and took her hand into mine. "Everything's going to be all right," I told her soothingly. She closed her eyes and sighed as if she really believed me. I remember wishing that I could believe it, too.

"Where is Geralyn?" I asked her.

"I think she had to work this afternoon," she told me.

It dawned on me then that my mother probably had no real idea of where Geralyn was at any given moment of that day—or any other.

"Well, I think I'll stop by and see her," I said, trying hard not to betray my full intent of giving my little sister a substantial piece of my mind.

"She'd like that," she murmured.

I wouldn't have bet on it.

Driving through town that afternoon, I noticed for the first time how much commerce had affected Cold Harbor. Not only was there a brand-new shopping center with new department stores, a giant video chain outlet, and a flurry of fast-food establishments, but new housing developments had cropped up everywhere—giving the deceptive impression that the town had grown and changed. One step into the video store burst that bubble very quickly, though.

Behind the counter beside my sister were two other long-time Cold Harbor residents, both of whom had married directly out of high school and had immediately begun to have children.

Some things never change, I reminded myself before approaching the counter.

"Audra, what are you doing here?" Geralyn asked with an accusing tone.

"Our mother is in the hospital," I reminded her. "What do you think I'm doing here?"

She glared at me in that little-sister way she'd always had, looking for all the world like she was going to prop her hands on her hips and begin tapping her foot any minute.

"How did you find out?" she wanted to know.

"Mrs. Walters called me," I informed her. I held back the urge to demand why I hadn't heard it directly from her. "Can you take a break? I'd like to talk to you before I go back to the hospital."

One of the two women standing behind the desk with her nodded, and Geralyn begrudgingly stepped out from behind the register.

"Let's go outside so we can have some privacy," she said pointedly.

The moment we got outside, I turned to her angrily. "What I need is to know what's going on at home?" I told her sternly. "Mom is a mess. And Mrs. Walters says that you're never home with her."

"That old busybody," Geralyn snapped.

"Geralyn, I'm worried," I said. "She's not doing well, and she can't be left alone all the time."

"Well, I have a life, too, Audra. Are you asking me to give it up to play baby-sitter to our mother?"

"Yes," I admitted. "Maybe I am. At least, in part."

"Well, forget it," she muttered.

I was so angry with her, I wanted to scream. But I'd known Geralyn since the day she was born, and the one thing that had never changed in all those years was her rebellious spirit. If I had said black, she would have fought to the death for white. If I'd said to stop, she would have gone, and she'd have left a hailstorm in her wake.

"Geralyn, I live almost five hours away. You're right here in town. For heaven's sake, you live in the same house with her, and you don't pay a dollar for room or board. Is it too much to ask that you make sure she's eating something every day and getting her medication on time?"

"She's a big girl, Audra," she told me.

"She was a big girl. Now she's an old woman. And she needs care," I reminded her.

"Then I guess you'd better think about moving back to Cold Harbor to help me give it to her then, huh?" she asked sarcastically.

There it was: My sister had finally voiced the most profound fear I'd ever had—one that I'd carried with me since the day that I'd left town.

"Geralyn, please. Work with me here," I begged.

"Oooh," she squealed. "You've just got to check this guy out."

I shot her a disgusted grimace, then casually turned toward the object of her attention.

Suddenly, the most gorgeous pair of legs I'd ever seen in blue jeans slid out of the driver's side of a sporty car. I felt a lump rise into my throat, and it thudded along with the slam of his door.

"Audra?" he asked.

My heart pounded out a savage beat against the wall of my chest. Did I know that guy? Geralyn's narrowed eyes let me know that she was wondering the same thing.

"Yes?" I answered hesitantly.

"Audra Hartman?" he asked as he slowly walked toward me, stopping just a foot away.

The shirt he was wearing seemed to bulge in all the right places, and it brought out the color of his sparkling eyes.

"Danny Beaumont," he told me. "From high school? We graduated together, remember?"

"Oh," I gasped. He'd grown into something unbelievable! "Danny Beaumont! How have you been?"

"I've been doing well. I'm an engineer."

"An engineer," I repeated with a nod. "That's great."

"What about you?" he asked casually.

"I'm with a public relations firm in New York," I answered.

"New York," he said slowly, as if he were weighing it out. "That's great. What are you doing back in Cold Harbor?"

"Our mother is in the hospital," I told him, and he looked at me strangely.

"Geralyn is your sister?" he asked, obviously surprised.

"Yes," I admitted.

I was surprised when a bit of envy registered inside me at the thought that my little sister obviously knew Danny Beaumont.

"Are you two friends?" I inquired, too casually.

"He's my favorite customer," Geralyn crooned, shooting Danny a flirtatious smile.

"No social life." Danny shrugged. "It lends itself to getting to know all of the most important people in town. The video rental people, the pizza delivery guys."

"And here I thought I was special," Geralyn interjected, a mock pout on her pretty face that instantly took me back to our childhood. She'd always been able to get just about whatever she wanted with just that one look.

Danny smiled at Geralyn, then returned his attention to me. "So, how long will you be home?"

"I'm not really sure," I explained, ignoring the familiar click of Geralyn's tongue. The one that meant she wasn't going to stand for the attention being off her for very long. "It depends on what the doctors say over the next few days."

"I'd love to take you to dinner while you're here," he suggested hopefully. "If you can swing the time."

"I'd really like that," I told him, pivoting my body slightly to avert Geralyn's glare. "Let me see how things go at the hospital. Can I get back to you?"

"You bet," he replied as he produced a business card from the pocket of his shirt. "Give me a call at my office."

"I will," I promised.

"Geralyn," he asked, causing my sister to brighten considerably, "would you slip these in the return slot for me?"

She touched the top of his hand for a long moment, establishing eye contact and grinning like some sort of cat on the prowl before finally taking the DVD cases from him with a nod.

"Absolutely," she told him. "I guess I'll see you Friday night."

"Geralyn and I have a standing date," he commented to me.

"You lead a very exciting life, Danny," I teased.

"Hey, Geralyn hooks me up with movies, microwave popcorn, and even the occasional box of candy," he joked.

"It's good to see you again, Danny," I told him honestly.

"You, too. If you're still in town this Friday, maybe you can save me from my boring self."

I smiled, concealing the hopefulness that had risen up from the very tips of my toes.

"Take care." He waved to Geralyn before sliding back behind the wheel of his car and backing out of the lot.

"Don't even think about it!" Geralyn exclaimed sardonically before I even had a chance to turn back to our conversation. "You are not going out with Danny Beaumont."

"He's just an old school friend, Geralyn. Unless—you two aren't actually dating, are you?" Of course, I knew that they weren't. I was only making the simple point that she had no real stake on Danny Beaumont's territory, and no right to tell me who I could or could not have dinner with.

"I've been working on him for a month," she warned. "You're not going to waltz back into town for a week and snatch him away from me."

"It's just dinner, little sister," I said breezily.

"Oh, no, it's not!" she cried. "You are not going out to dinner or anything else with him, Audra!"

"Look, we need to talk about Mom," I reminded her.

"What about her?" she asked. "She'll be fine. It was just a little accident."

71

"Have you seen her?" I asked incredulously. "She's totally bruised. She has stitches in her head, and a sprained wrist."

"It was an accident—" she began.

"And even if this hadn't have happened, she's in no shape to care for herself on a daily basis, Geralyn. We've got to figure something out."

"I told you before," she said firmly. "I'm not going to become the full-time nurse. If you want to take on that job, be my guest. But I'm not going to do it."

Frustration held back every foul word that I wanted to utter in anger. My sister had always been able to choke me up like that. Some things just never changed.

"I'm going back to the hospital," I stated in defeat. "We'll talk more over dinner. What time do you get off?"

"Six," she answered. "But I'm going out tonight."

"Geralyn, please. Change your plans and have dinner with me. Help me figure this out?" I begged.

"Oh, all right. Where will you take me?" she asked.

"I'll cook. Whatever you want."

"What I want is to go out," she said. "I'll come home and change, and then you can take me to Randalo's."

It wasn't a name I recognized, but knowing my sister I felt certain that Randalo's was the most expensive restaurant in town. But, if that was what I was going to have to do to work everything out, so be it.

"Randalo's it is," I promised.

Dinner with my sister was every bit as frustrating and excruciating as I'd expected it to be. Conversation about my mother continuously turned into how things related to Geralyn, and then, into long, rambling attempts at impressing me with her tales of parties, dancing, man-hunts, and conquests. When Danny Beaumont popped into the conversation, I understood much more about Geralyn's interest in him. It wasn't just those sexy legs and engaging smile that had snagged her attention. In her eyes, Danny symbolized the potential for a better life—an easier life.

"He's got a great job, and he drives a cool car," she nearly swooned. "He's got miles more to offer than any of the other guys in this town. So keep your hands off him."

I let her believe that I had ignored her high command, but the notion did register that she wasn't entirely off base. Danny had matured into someone confident and engaging. He'd grown into himself, in a way, and he'd become far different from the somewhat awkward high school student I'd once known.

Nothing much was accomplished that night besides a huge restaurant bill, and I spent the sleepless night that followed in the

72

house alone. Geralyn had gone out after our dinner, and she didn't return home until nearly five in the morning. I finally dozed off around then, and awoke the next morning to a kitchen littered with dirty dishes and empty beer cans. Geralyn and her anonymous companion were still sleeping upstairs when I left the house at around noon.

After a quick visit with my mom at the hospital, I took a drive around town. The old school had grown. Even though the main building looked pretty much the same, the high school campus was more spread out, with several new buildings added to the property.

When my stomach began to growl around three, I remembered that I hadn't eaten anything since dinner with my sister the evening before, and I pulled up in front of Hugh's Hamburger Shack with a taste for one of his juicy burgers and a chocolate shake.

"Audra!" I heard someone call.

I spotted Danny the moment I walked through the door, and I approached his table with an excited smile that I tried to suppress into mere cordiality. He certainly had changed since high school. I'd remembered him as a bit on the nerdy side, always with his head in a book at the library. Our circles of friends had been very different in those days, and the thought of dating him wouldn't have ever occurred to me back then. Suddenly, however, I looked at him and saw a handsome, finely developed man.

"Sneaking out of the office in the middle of the day?" I asked him, glancing down at the half-empty shake on the table before him.

"A guy just has to have a shake every once in a while!" he teased. "What are you doing here?"

"Well, a girl needs her share of shakes, too," I teased.

He returned my smile. "Join me?"

From the moment I sat down, things were relaxed and easy with Danny. Conversation came naturally, and we talked about everything from old high school acquaintances, to my life in New York, to our shared enthusiasm for baseball. When the topic rolled around to my mother, it didn't seem out of the ordinary in the least to confide my concerns to him.

"I'm at a loss," I told him finally. "I can't just leave town and let her continue to fend for herself. And yet, I don't want to walk away from my life in New York. I love it there."

"What about your sister?" he asked. "She's here to pick up the slack, isn't she?"

How in the world was I supposed to respond to that?

"Geralyn has a very full life," I began cautiously. "Becoming a nursemaid to my mother at this point in her young life doesn't exactly have a great appeal. And I can't say that I blame her."

I silently wondered why I was being so protective of Geralyn. Why didn't I just tell him the real truth, which was that Geralyn and I had been engaged in some unnamed competition ever since I could remember?

She had been the wild one, the free spirit; and I had been the sensible daughter, the one my parents had never had to concern themselves with. I'd made good grades and aspired toward a career, while Geralyn was creative and funny, with a wild streak that attracted an endless array of male suitors. We were as different as could be, seemingly relieved not to be caught in the other's tide of attributes. And yet, each of us had always seemed to resent the other for those same qualities. It was sibling rivalry in its finest form—a story as old as time.

"So, you're going to be the nursemaid instead? That hardly seems fair," Danny commented, unaware of the drift my thoughts had taken.

"Oh, I don't know, Danny. There has to be an answer here. I just can't, for the life of me, figure out what it could be," I admitted.

"Well," he began, thinking carefully about his next words. "What are you thinking about doing next? Is moving back something that you're even considering?"

"Considering?" I repeated. "Yes. I'd be lying if I didn't admit to that, just because of my mom's current condition. But, do I want to do it? Absolutely not."

"You always did have that dream of escaping Cold Harbor," he remarked, and it took me by surprise.

"How did you know that? We weren't exactly friends in high school," I reminded him.

"No." He grinned. "But you didn't make it a secret how you felt about this little town. You were too big for Cold Harbor—you always were. Everyone knew that you'd break free the moment you saw your chance."

"A lot of people broke free, Danny. But it seems as though they've all been lassoed back again."

The town always had come with its own built-in expectations of its young women, and I'd rebelled against the mandate at a very young age. I remembered imagining that in cities all across the country, high school graduations had meant new beginnings and the opportunity for dreams realized. But, in Cold Harbor, I realized that caps and gowns were quickly traded in for aprons and infant car seats.

The term "career" really had meant contributing to the family unit, and the other girls that I'd known had moved blissfully into retail jobs or behind various reception desks, biding their time until the big white wedding and subsequent arrival of the first of several crying babies.

Even when they had managed to escape such a fate for the exciting life of college or a big-city job, they'd always seemed to return to Cold Harbor. And, with the return of each escapee, my determination had surged with new resolve. The drudgery of a provincial life just wasn't for me, and I peeled out of town in my convertible just three days after graduation, determined never to come back, except for the occasional holiday visit.

"If that's how you see it," he told me seriously, "then I don't think you'd be doing your mom any big favors by coming back. Not if you'd be miserable."

I thought about that for a long moment. But, what were my alternatives?

"What would I even do?" I asked him. "It's not like I can get the kind of job I have in New York here in Cold Harbor."

"You're in public relations," he recalled. "You know, I think we have an opening at my company in the public relations department. If you'd be interested, I could put in a good word for you."

"Really?" I asked him. "Well, that would be one good thing. At least, I wouldn't have to worry about looking for work."

Danny reached across the table and took my hand in his. "I have to admit, it wouldn't break my heart to have you around town for a while," he said softly. "It is so good to see you again, Audra. You've matured into a really beautiful woman. I'd like the chance to get to know you better."

"I'd like that, too," I admitted. "If I stay."

Those last words seemed to change the whole expression on Danny's face. Suddenly, his expression was one of disappointment mixed with embarrassment.

Perhaps he'd thought I'd been looking down my nose at Cold Harbor and all of the small-town types who lived there. If I'd actually sounded like that, I hadn't meant to. But, I had to admit that, in comparison to New York, Cold Harbor was a little backward in my views. It was, after all, the town I'd always dubbed "Most Likely To Run Away From."

"It's something to think about," I added with a smile that he finally returned.

And then, the old churning in my stomach began again. Once again, I became suffused with that familiar fear of becoming one of the masses, drawn helplessly back to the place from which we'd sworn we would flee. The place to where we would never return—no matter what.

And yet, there I was. Eating a burger, drinking a chocolate shake, and holding hands with Danny Beaumont. It was as if I were caught in the middle of a very bad dream, one where I was doomed to relive my teenaged years.

Wow, God really does have a sense of humor, I thought. Now I know why they say you should never say "never again."

I was humming some old song from the past when I stepped into line at the supermarket, my arms brimming with more groceries than I'd originally intended to buy. Suddenly, a voice from behind me joined in on the chorus, and I reeled around to find Cecily Hunter standing behind me. Cecily had been my best friend all through high school, but over the years, we'd drifted away into just sending one another greeting cards at the holidays.

"Audra?" she squealed when I turned around, and she came at me with the kind of force that prompted me to drop my groceries onto the counter.

"Cecily, I can't believe it! I was just thinking last night about calling you!" I exclaimed.

"Then, why didn't you? How long are you in town? How have you been?" she asked breathlessly.

"Uh, it was too late to call," I told her, rolling my eyes upward as I weeded through her questions. "I'm not sure how long I'll be staying. And, I'm fine—just fine. How about you?"

"It's so good to see you again," she said, hugging me a second time. "But I hate you! You just never age a day."

I wrote that off as one of those things old friends say, then moved forward in the line. "How are Dave and the kids?"

"Everyone is great. I know that Dave would love to see you. Can you make it over for dinner?" she asked eagerly.

I hadn't realized it until she'd issued the invitation, but I knew instantly that Cecily was just the sort of distraction that I'd been needing—not to mention a perfect excuse not to spend another evening alone at the house.

"Really?" I asked hopefully. "I would love that."

Dinner at the Hunters' was like something out of an old black-and-white sitcom on television—all of her four kids talking at once and vying for attention while Mom and Dad sat at opposite ends of the table, presiding skillfully over the chaos. It provoked more than a couple of twinges inside of my stomach.

Cecily was a great mother, and her perfect little family unit inspired admiration as well as a bit of envy. Watching her reminded me of all that I'd been missing in the life that I'd managed to cram full with the details and obligations of a working girl.

"You and Dave have made such a great life for yourselves here, Cecily," I told her as we worked together in her tidy little kitchen, cleaning up the dinner dishes.

"I can't complain," she commented as she handed me the last of the glasses she'd dried. I placed it in the cabinet. "But then, I often do."

I giggled at that, and she whipped her dish towel at me with a snap.

"What about you, Audra? Are you seeing anyone special in New York?" she asked.

"I've had no time," I told her, trying to remind myself that it was the truth, but feeling conspicuously like I'd just uttered one of those lines people used to make an excuse for the choices they'd made.

"When I first saw you in line at the market," Cecily admitted, "I was so hoping that you were going to tell me you were moving back to town."

"No," I said with a sigh as we took our places back at the table. "Mom's in the hospital, and Geralyn is as much help as she ever was, so I'm just here trying to sort things out."

"Geralyn," she said with only the slightest hint of a groan. "Is she still working over at the video store?"

"Yes, she is. She rents videos by day and lives the wild life at night."

"So I've heard." She shook her head.

I wanted to ask Cecily what she meant by that—to get some details on my younger sister's budding reputation—but two of her four children chose just that moment to burst into the room, crawling all over their mother and fussing about the others' monopoly on the television set. We never got back to the subject, but I supposed, on the drive home, that it had been just as well. Some things, though known for certain in theory, were often better left unproven.

The next few days were filled with hospital visits and walks by the water to think. But those introspective sessions made me feel a little bit like a hamster caught on the spinning wheel of its metal cage. No matter what, they always came back full circle to the idea of giving up what I'd fought so hard to attain. In order to help my mother, I'd have to take three giant steps backward into the life I'd run from at the first opportunity that'd come along.

Trying to be a good daughter, however, I did take that meeting with Calvin Brooks over at Danny's company, and we discussed at great length the possibility of a position in the public relations department. The conversation was amiable enough and resulted in a job offer right there on the spot. But, despite the surprisingly adequate salary and competitive benefits package included in the offer, there was one thing that he just couldn't throw in to sweeten the deal: Another location.

"What is it that's holding you back?" Danny asked me one evening over dinner at Randalo's, a place I'd actually taken to quite nicely, despite the fact that my sister liked it so much.

"Cold Harbor," I told him in earnest. "That's really it. I just don't want to come crawling back with my tail between my legs to the hometown that sent me packing to begin with."

"What did you do?" he asked curiously.

"What do you mean, what did I do?" I was confused by the question.

"Well," he said, chuckling, "you tell the story as if you were run out of town on a rail. Did you rob the stagecoach? Blow up the bank? Insult the sheriff?"

"Oh, please," I said with the wave of my hand. "You know what I mean."

"I guess I do," he admitted. "I'm just trying to understand it."

We'd been over the subject at least a half a dozen times since our first meeting over milk shakes. Danny Beaumont knew very good and well how I felt about Cold Harbor, and he knew how hard it had been for me to make my escape. He also knew just how devoted to the cause of staying away I had become.

"Is it really so bad?" he asked me. "Are there chemicals in the water that make you fear for the safety of your future children?"

"Quit being so dramatic," I warned.

"I could say the same thing to you," he told me as he took my hand. "You were a child when you decided that this place was so horrible and backward, Audra. You're a woman now. Surely you can see that it's not so terrible to make a life in a small town."

"Hey, what's the big secret?"

We both looked up and were startled to find Geralyn standing over us.

"Can I join you, or is this some secret conversation that you wouldn't want your little sister to overhear?" she asked.

"Of course," Danny was first to say. "Join us."

Geralyn wasted no time in nodding at the hostess and, when a waiter provided a third chair for the table, she pulled it conspicuously close to Danny before plopping down into it and slipping her arm around his shoulder.

"You know, I never would have pegged you for the type who would go after someone like Audra," she told him.

"No?" he asked her seriously. "And why not?"

"Well, she's so serious. And stuffy. I'd have thought that you were more the type to enjoy having a little fun—if given the opportunity."

"Thank-you," I interjected sarcastically. I'd always known that I could count on my little sister to be the one to pull my skirt up around my head or to dip my ponytail in the inkwell—if only figuratively.

"Well, come on," Geralyn said to me. "You have to admit you're not the more thrill-seeking of the Hartman sisters!"

There were so many things I could have said in reply that my brain nearly froze from overload. Instead, I decided to let the comment pass and bit down on my tongue. If Danny hadn't been present, however, I surely wouldn't have managed such restraint.

"I think you both have your virtues," Danny told us. Then, he looked pointedly at my sister. "I happen to find Audra's company fascinating."

"Fascinating?" she repeated in disbelief. "Well, there's a word, I suppose. But if you ever get tired of her and want to trade her in for someone a little more energetic—"

"I'm sure he'll know where to find you, Geralyn," I interrupted, and it was just about all I could do not to add a few possible off-colored suggestions.

"Would you like to order some dinner?" Danny asked quickly, obviously intent on changing the subject. "We've just ordered ours a few minutes ago."

While Danny flagged down the waiter and Geralyn coyly debated over the various selections on the menu, I just focused on breathing. And, on ignoring the dozen or so flips of her hair which always seemed to accompany some form of bodily contact with Danny. It was one of the longest-lasting and worst-tasting meals of my life, and I couldn't even have said what it was that I'd ordered. Danny, of course, was Geralyn's choice for main entree, as well as her planned dessert.

Just as we were about to prepare to leave, I looked up in time to spot Cecily and Dave walking through the front entrance. Cecily was waving her arms and grinning in that way she had about her. She could light up an entire room with that enthusiastic smile.

"Do you remember Cecily?" I asked Danny as they approached the table, and he rose to his feet immediately.

"Of course I do," he said, bending down to kiss Cecily's cheek. As he shook Dave's hand, Danny turned back to me. "Dave and I are foursome buddies down at the golf course."

"How funny," I replied. "What a small world."

"Way too small, if you ask me," Geralyn whispered in my direction. Then, she stood up and looked at me sourly. "I'm going. I'll see you later at home."

Before making her grand exit, Geralyn paused to give Danny an embrace that was way too intimate. "Don't you forget what I said now, Danny," she said softly, but not so softly that we couldn't all hear her. "When you grow tired of my sister, call me and we can discuss an upgrade."

Danny good-naturedly guided Geralyn on her way, but Cecily's expression was one of clear disdain.

"So," she whispered as she gave me a little hug. "You and Danny, huh?"

"It's just dinner, Cecily," I assured her.

"My life with Dave started with a meal, Audra. But you keep an eye on that sister of yours, would you? Or else, she'll eat poor Danny alive."

"Our table's ready," Dave said to her, and Cecily waved a quick good-bye as she followed his lead.

"You'll come over for dinner again very soon," she remarked over her shoulder. "And next time, Danny, you'll come along."

That evening with Geralyn had been just one more checkmark on the long list of reasons why returning to Cold Harbor on a permanent basis held no appeal for me whatsoever. The next morning, I placed a phone call to Calvin Brooks.

"I'm sorry to hear that," he commented when I told him I had chosen not to accept his offer of employment.

"It's a very generous offer," I told him honestly. "And if I were going to stay in Cold Harbor, it would probably be ideal. But, I'm really only here for as long as it takes to get my mom through this crisis. After that, I've decided to return to my life in New York."

"I understand," he replied. "But if anything changes, please do give us a call again."

"Thank you, Mr. Brooks," I said.

Even as I replaced the receiver to the cradle of the telephone, though, I knew that I wouldn't be making that call. Cold Harbor just didn't fit in with any of the plans that I'd been so carefully making over the years.

Danny Beaumont, though—now, he was another thing entirely. He had all the qualities I'd ever hoped to find in a man. He was easygoing and kind, sweet and funny, and he sure wasn't hard on the eyes—not even in the brightest sun. But, was he enough to draw me back to Cold Harbor?

I wasn't certain that anything held that kind of magnetic appeal for me. But if anything or anyone would have been able to tempt me, I knew that Danny Beaumont was the one who'd have been able to do it.

The idea of moving back to Cold Harbor, no matter how noble the purpose, was daunting, to say the least. My mom was aging fast, and Geralyn, was no help at all in planning her care. I knew that I had to do something.

I'd come to town on an emergency visit. My mom had been hospitalized after a pretty bad fall, and of course, I'd run into Danny again. What I hadn't counted on was my immediate attraction to him. It had been so overpowering that it had definitely succeeded in taking a bit of the sting out of the notion of uprooting the life that I'd made in New York in order to move back to the hometown that I'd escaped gladly.

In my heart, I knew that I didn't want to move back—not permanently, anyway. So, I'd taken a leave of absence from my job. I'd be gone just a month or so—that was what I'd promised them. I'd packed up as few essentials as I could possibly manage, and then, I'd headed home. Taking up residence in my old room, I'd known that I was too old to be living the life of a high school girl, but yet, it'd seemed as though I'd still fit into the burger shop scene with a strange sort of ease.

Despite the not-so-subtle objections of my sister, who was carrying her own sort of torch for Danny, I started seeing him socially on a fairly regular basis. In between doctor's appointments, trying to plan healthy meals, and administering Mom's medication on a timely basis, Danny filled those days in Cold Harbor with lovely diversions.

We went on picnics, rode bike rides around the park, and explored wooded trails on horseback. Danny updated me on all of the strides that my little hometown had made, introduced me to the new restaurants, and touted often the benefits of small-town life. There was no mistaking his hope that, come the end of the month, I would decide to stay. But, the idea that Cold Harbor was a trap to be avoided at all costs was one that had been deeply ingrained in my personality from a very young age, and it wasn't an easy obstacle for me to overcome.

And then there was the issue of my sister—Geralyn.

Although she was very much the typical small-town party animal, with a different date for every occasion, Geralyn had set her sights on Danny long before I'd ever come back to town. Seeing his interest in me growing hadn't been an easy thing for her to take, and she'd seized upon every opportunity to remind me of that fact.

"You have no loyalty," she accused. "There is supposed to be a certain code of conduct between sisters, but you don't care about that. You think only of yourself."

In a way, I supposed that she was right. But, Danny's affections were obviously directed at me and not my sister; and what was worse was that I had begun feeling something for him as well. What we were experiencing were very real emotions between two adults, I rationalized to myself again and again. Not the young fantasies of a girl who was much too young—as well as entirely wrong—for him, anyway.

I supposed that there was a small part of me that gloated over his attraction to me instead of my sister. Geralyn had always been the focal point of any male attention that had surfaced in or around our adolescence, and for once in my life, the focus was on me instead. The teenage competition and typical sibling rivalry that had run wild in our youth had apparently surfaced into the present, and the residue had brought an additional glimmer to the affection that had begun building between Danny and me.

"Geralyn is a beautiful girl," Danny told me one night when we stopped in for coffee after a late-night showing of a revival at the old movie theater in town. "I won't lie to you. I might have asked her out one day, if you hadn't have come back to town. But, the fact is, you have. And it's you that I'm interested in, Audra. It's you that I'm falling for."

I wouldn't have admitted it out loud, but my ego had taken a huge leap at that admission. Geralyn always had been the younger, prettier, and more adventurous sister, and having someone like Danny choose me had done wonders for my self-esteem. The fact of the matter was, however, that I had no plans of staying on in Cold Harbor. I was there to care for my mother, and Danny was just an added bonus to my time there. A little nagging sense of guilt at the back of my mind kept reminding me that the day would come when I would return to New York, and he would remain behind. And so would Geralyn.

For right now, though, I thought, I'll just enjoy every moment that I have with him.

But, lives were never so uncomplicated, were they? And why should mine have been any different?

The weeks that Danny and I spent together were almost magical. For a woman who hadn't ever really allowed herself to believe in the whole Prince Charming myth, I had begun to feel a little bit like Cinderella. The wicked stepsister in my fairy tale did everything she could to divert the prince's attentions, but he had eyes for me alone—and I loved it.

One afternoon, soon after Mom had been released for home care, Danny brought a picnic lunch over to the house. It was something just like leading men did in the movies—a wicker basket all packed up with fried chicken, potato salad, fruit, and a decadent chocolate cake. He even draped a checkered tablecloth across the coffee table in the living room, and he rolled my mom's wheelchair right up to it to join us while we sat cross-legged on the floor.

"You two look just as natural as can be," Mom commented happily, and I could see from the look in her eyes that the hope was there that Danny would be just the draw I'd need to keep me at home. "You look as though you just belong together."

"There's a good reason for that." Danny grinned. "I really believe that we do belong together."

I was sure that I blushed when he leaned over and planted a kiss right on my mouth—right there in front of my mom and God.

"It's not going to be easy to leave," I felt compelled to add, and I saw the glimmer of hopefulness fade in my mother's eyes. I didn't dare look over at Danny at that moment, but I felt pretty certain that he'd been splashed as well. As it turned out, he proved me right later that afternoon.

"Do you mind if I borrow her for a while?" Danny asked Mom after he'd cleared up the leftovers from our indoor picnic.

"Certainly not." She smiled conspiratorially. "I'd like to take a rest, anyway. You two kids enjoy yourselves."

Danny and I walked hand in hand down the path to the beach. It had become second nature for us to head in that direction, and we had a favorite spot that we always seemed to gravitate toward.

"Audra," he said as we settled down on a bench. "We need to talk about something."

I firmly believe that nothing good had ever followed that statement. "Okay," I said with a sigh, knowing full well where we were headed.

"You mentioned returning to New York," he began.

"Well, Danny, we always knew—"

"I know, I know," he interrupted, waving his hand to stop me from my usual speech. "You've made no secret about your plans. I was just wondering if there was anything firm in the works."

"I don't know what you mean," I said innocently.

"Have you set a date for when you'll be leaving?" he asked casually, but the seriousness in the question surrounded us like a thick fog.

"I'm thinking about the end of next week," I responded honestly. "Mom's home, and she's doing better. The insurance will cover an in-home nurse to check on her several times a week for the next few weeks after I leave, so I don't have to worry about her."

"What about us?" he asked. "Do you worry about us?"

I turned to look at him, and I couldn't even say what it was that brought the tears so quickly into my eyes. I didn't want to leave him. But, Cold Harbor just wasn't my home anymore. It hadn't been an easy road, but I'd made a life for myself in New York, and I wanted that life back.

"Maybe you could come up and visit me," I suggested hopefully. "There are lots of things to do in the city. We could have such a wonderful time."

"I don't doubt it." But the emotion that I detected in the words, though, contradicted any actual possibilities I might have been able to imagine. In answer to my unspoken question, Danny shook his head. "No, Audra. I won't be coming to visit you in New York," he told me sadly.

A person's eardrums could have shattered in the stillness that followed. "Why?" I asked softly.

"I've fallen in love with you," he admitted, then tenderly grazed the line of my jaw with one finger. "I never thought I could feel this way about a woman again."

"Then, why not come to New York?" I asked. "And, of course, sometimes I'll come here."

"Why would we do that?" He looked confused, and I remember feeling as if I wanted to laugh out loud. Thankfully, I didn't.

"This is my home," he finally continued. "I've always known that this was where I was going to live."

"And I've always known that I wouldn't live here," I countered.

"That's what I'm saying. So, what do we do—visit on weekends for the rest of our lives? Knowing full well that neither one of us is ever going to make the change required to be with the other?"

"What are we going to do?" I asked cautiously, not really wanting to hear his answer.

"We're going to be realistic about our situation," he told me. "And we're going to be honest with each other. I don't know about you, but I'm going to hurt over what comes next for a long, long time to come. But, when the day comes that you pack up your car and go back to New York, we're going to say good-bye."

I was sobbing then. I didn't even try to hold back my tears. Danny wrapped his arms around me. He held me and rocked me as I cried, and neither one of us spoke another word for a really long time. I didn't tell him that my heart was breaking right inside of me.

I could hardly bear the idea of spending the rest of my life knowing that I had finally found the person I wanted to live with forever, but knowing, too, that I just couldn't live with him in Cold Harbor. And, I'd never told Danny that I loved him, too. Although I did love him—almost more than I could stand.

The days that followed were different than the others had been. It was as if that little talk we'd had at the beach was a barrier which separated love from pain. And, when I finally left Cold Harbor the following week, I did so knowing that the magic I'd found with Danny was surely over.

Getting back into the swing of my life in New York wasn't as difficult as I'd imagined it would be. There was the daily grind of my job to get back into, and of course, all those dust bunnies that were littering my apartment had to be chased away. It only hurt significantly at night, when the apartment fell silent and I was left with nothing more than my own thoughts to keep me company. Sleep was an elusive adversary.

Every so often when I would call home, Mom would mention Danny in passing. She would say that Geralyn had seen him at the video store, or she'd relate that he had dropped by with some flowers and a short visit to cheer her. After a couple of months, I was at least able to hear his name without my heart pounding wildly, and I was even able to remember our times together without being overwhelmed with the compulsion to weep over the loss or write some really bad poetry. I'd even accepted a date now and then, none of which had amounted to anything—but, I had to believe that there was still hope.

When Mom's birthday approached, convincing myself that I was ready to face Cold Harbor again, I suggested a visit to her on one of our morning telephone talks.

"Oh, I don't think that's such a very good idea," she murmured uncharacteristically. "I'm not so sure that the timing is right for you to come back just now."

"What does that mean?" I asked with a laugh. "Don't you want to see me?"

"Of course I do, honey," she replied, but something in her voice told me to drop the subject. Something was going on in Cold Harbor that my mother was trying to keep from me. The element of surprise suddenly revealed itself as the only possibility of my finding out just what it was.

And so, I changed the subject to vague topics such as the weather. Then, I asked if there was anything that she needed, and finally, I ended the conversation quickly.

"I love you, Mom," I told her.

She returned the sentiment, and I hung up the phone, standing very still and staring straight ahead at the tiny scrape on my kitchen wall.

"Not the right time to come home," I repeated out loud. "What in the world does that mean?"

A few days later, I was in my car, an overnight backpack stuffed with just enough clothes for the weekend, driving toward Cold Harbor. But, the moment I walked in the door, my questioning was silenced. The first glimpse of family life I'd witnessed had explained my mother's hesitation immediately.

"What are you doing here?" Geralyn cried as she turned from the sink and faced me, her belly just as round as it could be.

"You're pregnant?" I stammered.

Geralyn's hands moved instantly to her stomach, and she held the little mound as she looked at me, wide-eyed.

"Answer me," she persisted, more softly now. "What are you doing here?"

"I came to surprise Mom," I told her, my eyes glued to her belly and my heartbeat thundering in my ears. "For her birthday."

"Oh," she murmured.

That was all she could say? "Geralyn! You're pregnant," I said, shocked.

"Yes," she admitted.

"How far along are you?" I asked hesitantly.

"A few months," she said.

"Why didn't you tell me?" I walked toward her slowly, as if preparing to examine some unexplainable phenomenon that had just dropped suddenly into my mother's kitchen out of the sky. "Why didn't Mom tell me?"

"I asked her not to," she explained.

"But, why?" I asked again.

"It's Danny's baby," she told me. "And we're getting married."

She could have told me that she'd been impregnated by an alien being from another planet, and I would have been less stunned.

"Danny?" I repeated.

"It wasn't anything that we planned," she hastened to tell me. "It just happened. Neither one of us ever expected anything like this to happen—or to feel as we do, Audra. I swear, it wasn't anything that we planned, but it happened. Suddenly, there's a baby to think about. When Danny asked me to marry him, I said yes. And then—"

Geralyn droned on—I really couldn't say for how long. I couldn't hear the words anymore over the roaring in my ears. I truly believed that I might have fainted if not for the fact that my own adrenaline was working so hard to coarse through my body.

"You're marrying Danny?" I asked, still too shocked to totally comprehend what she'd told me.

My brain ached from all the questions. When had it happened? And how? I recalled Danny telling me that he might have asked Geralyn out, had he never met me. But, he had met me, and he'd fallen in love with me. At least, that was what he had said.

Geralyn was still talking when I turned on my heels and walked right back out of the house. I had to talk to Danny. I had to hear it from his lips.

"Mr. Beaumont is on a conference call right now," his secretary said, when I got to his office, but I wasn't able to process the information.

I just walked right on past her into Danny's office and stood over his desk. The way he looked up at me, with the telephone propped on his shoulder and his mouth hanging open, you'd have thought that I was a ghost who'd come back from the dead.

"Can I get back to you?" he asked the caller on the other end of the receiver, never once taking his eyes from mine. "Something's come up on this end."

He hadn't even replaced the phone to its cradle when I'd started talking. "You plan on marrying my sister?" I asked coldly.

"She's going to have a baby, Audra," he said as he rounded the desk, but the moment he placed his hand on my shoulder, I shook myself loose from his touch. It was as if I'd been jolted with an electrical shock.

"You slept with Geralyn, Danny? When? How long was I gone before you slept with my sister?" I was so filled with fury that I could barely speak.

"I was heartbroken when you left," he told me, but everything inside of me had grown instantly cold. I couldn't believe him. I wouldn't.

"Geralyn was a comfort to me in those first weeks," he went on. "She was a good friend when I needed one badly."

"The only person that Geralyn knows how to be a good friend to is herself," I snapped. "How could you do this? I thought—I thought that you loved me."

"I do love you, Audra," he said softly, but I slapped his hand away as he reached out for my face. "I still do."

"You love me so much," I retorted bitterly, "that you're going to marry my sister."

"That hasn't been decided," he admitted awkwardly. "But, she's carrying my child, Audra. What would you have me do?"

"It's not what I'd have you do now, Danny," I replied, my hands trembling violently as I reached for the door. "It's what I would have had you not do a few months ago."

"Audra, wait!" he pleaded.

"Good-bye, Danny. Best of luck to you and your future bride," I snapped.

I must have cried for two hours after that, right out in the parking lot, slumped over the steering wheel of my car. Even with the windows closed, I was sure that my wailing had drawn the attention of everyone in a hundred-yard radius. And, afterward, I'd never even bothered to pick up the bag that I'd left in the foyer of my mother's house. I'd just turned my car around and driven right back to New York.

There were five or six messages on my voice mail the next morning—a couple from Geralyn, another from my mom, two from Danny, and then, the final one from Cecily Hunter.

Just the sound of Cecily's voice pierced me straight through with betrayal. How could she have known what was going on and not have let me know? My own mother had been instrumental in covering up the truth, but at least she'd had her role as Geralyn's mother to fall back on. Her loyalty would have had to have been equally strained between her two daughters, but Cecily was a different story altogether. She was the one who had warned me about Geralyn and Danny to begin with.

"I'm so sorry that you found out the way you did," Cecily's message began. "I wanted to tell you. I'd planned to tell you. I just hadn't figured out how or when. Please, Audra. Call me," she begged.

Call her! If I'd have had it within me to laugh, I'd have done so right out loud at that. I had no intention of ever speaking to Cecily Hunter again. But, the message that she'd left on my voice mail a week later was enough to instantly break my resolve.

"It's your mom, Audra," she said softly. "She had a stroke this morning. And it doesn't look good."

No matter how I felt about Danny and Geralyn, and even Cecily, for the roles they'd played in the heartbreak that was still fresh in my mind, I knew that my mother needed me. And so, I made the trip back to Cold Harbor, that time using the long drive to wedge up the steel resolve to face them all again. When I arrived at the hospital, I walked through the door to my mother's room with a heart of stone and a face to match.

"Audra, she'll be so glad you're here," Danny told me, but I waltzed on past him as if he weren't even there.

I took my mother's hand and looked into her pain-filled eyes, and I lied as I promised her that everything was going to be all right. It felt as if nothing could ever be all right again.

"Are you ever going to talk to me again?" Geralyn asked the next morning when she came across me in the kitchen, pouring coffee into my mother's favorite mug.

"What would you like to talk about?" I asked her coolly.

"Danny and I have decided to get married this afternoon," she announced, and I wondered if it was true or just something that she'd hurled at me for maximum effect.

"I think that's a good idea," I replied. "A big wedding wouldn't be appropriate with Mom in the state that she's in. But the baby will need a father—and a name."

"That's all you have to say?" she asked incredulously.

"Will you be moving out of the house then?" I asked. "Moving in with your new husband?"

"Y-yes, I suppose I will," she stammered. It was the first sign of uncertainty that I could ever remember detecting in Geralyn. My nonhysteria over the situation seemed to be throwing her well off guard.

"I think that's best," I concluded.

Geralyn and Danny weren't married that afternoon, though, or on any other day. My presence had apparently spooked the father of her child, and he'd made excuses about waiting until Mom had recovered—until they could be sure it was the right thing for them both as well as for the baby.

The baby. I could hardly stand the words, even as they floated around inside my head.

The bottom line was that Geralyn and I were going to be living under the same roof, tripping over one another on a regular basis, and I would have the misfortune of watching Danny's baby grow inside of her daily.

I wanted to hate her, and hate the baby right along with her, but the revulsion didn't build the way that I had expected. In fact, as the weeks passed, I began to feel involved in the life of Geralyn's child. I found myself cooking healthy meals and researching prenatal needs, even picking up the occasional article of tiny clothing whenever I went to the mall. It was completely unbelievable to me, but Geralyn and I actually began to get closer. We had begun bonding over the existence of the little life inside her.

Danny hadn't been around in nearly two months, and one night, I mustered up the courage to ask Geralyn about him.

"He's very busy at work," she replied tersely.

I knew that there had to be more to it. Perhaps they were seeing one another more discreetly because of me, or perhaps she simply didn't want to share that part of her life with me, all things considered. Whatever the reason, I was determined not to inquire about Danny again—and I didn't.

A few weeks later, when everything began to run out in my life— money, resolve, and my New York employer's patience—I made a decision. It was perhaps the most difficult one of my life. The very weekend that Mom was admitted to a physical rehab center, I drove home to New York and loaded everything I owned into a moving van. Then, I drove it back to Cold Harbor.

I had a mother who needed me, and a pregnant sister who was little more than a child herself. There are only so many excuses a woman could make for not doing what she knew was the right thing, and I'd run out of them. Despite Danny, despite my steel-solid commitment never to return to Cold Harbor, and despite the fact that my sister was carrying the child of the man I loved right there under my nose, I called Danny's company and accepted the job offer that they'd extended.

And so, it was a certainty: I was moving home. Heaven help me.

Those next few weeks were a walking blur. I got settled in the house where I'd grown up, mingling the possessions of my independent city-dwelling life with those of my childhood. It was an odd sensation, coming home from my new job at the end of the day, cooking dinner for myself in what had always been my mother's kitchen, and then, climbing the stairs to the bedroom that had housed more teenaged angst and fits of hysteria than I cared to remember.

Every night, I would slip beneath the comforter that I'd bought during my first week in New York, and then, I'd snuggle down into the lumpy mattress of a bed that I'd been sleeping on since childhood. The dreams that touched me at night, when sleep finally did manage to find me, were tangled with threads from the distant past as well as swatches of fabric from the more current present. I'd done what I had always sworn that I would never do, and my psyche was as knotted up over it as my emotions were.

Mom was sent to a rehab center for a few weeks, which left Geralyn and I alone to face each other on a daily basis. Without Mom, there was nothing standing guard between us except the growing lump of baby in her stomach, and it was getting bigger every day.

One morning, as I was lingering over my coffee as an excuse to await her exit from the house, she cried out in a way that crumpled all of my defenses and left them in a heap on the kitchen floor as I flew past them and to her side.

"What is it?" I asked without hesitation.

"The baby," she replied, her face contorted in pain.

"Is something wrong?" I asked anxiously.

"I don't know," she answered. Then, she let out a second scream. She stretched her hand out toward mine, and I took it without a thought.

"Tell me, Geralyn," I prompted.

"Something's not right," she told me, looking at me in a way that brought to the surface every sisterly instinct I'd thought I'd sent packing months before. "It hurts."

"What does it feel like?" I asked.

"Like I'm being punished," she whispered hoarsely.

"Geralyn," I gently reprimanded.

"It feels like it's punching me," she went on.

I smiled, and I could see a glint of irritation in the relief that spread over her.

"The baby's kicking," I told her. "That's a good sign. It's time."

"Why?" she asked doubtfully.

"Because it means that the baby's healthy," I explained.

"No. I mean, why is it kicking me?" she went on.

"It's cranky. Just like its mommy," I teased.

"Very funny," she commented sarcastically. Then, she released my hand as if she'd only just realized that she'd been holding it.

"He's stretching," I told her softly, then smoothed back the hair at the side of her worried face. "He's growing bigger, and the quarters are a little cramped. That's all. It's natural," I assured her.

"Are you sure?" she asked. Suddenly, she sounded like a little girl herself—the baby sister that I'd always protected fiercely.

"Yes, I'm sure," I told her.

After a long moment of thought, she grinned. "Is that coffee I smell?" she asked.

"Yes," I answered.

"Can I have some?"

"No, you may not," I said firmly.

"Why not?" she asked incredulously.

"You can't be drinking caffeine right now, Geralyn. I'll make you some herbal tea, though," I suggested.

"I want coffee!" she demanded. She was still such a child. With all of her antics and adventures, Geralyn was more ready to be raised alongside of a baby than to be raising one herself. Suddenly, the whole situation struck me as very funny, and I began to giggle.

"Are you laughing at me?" she asked.

"No," I told her, trying hard to wipe the grin from my face.

"Yes, you are, Audra. You're making fun of me. And I don't think—"

"I'm not making fun of you," I interrupted. "Now, come on in the kitchen and I'll make you some breakfast and a cup of herbal tea."

"I hate that stuff," she muttered. Still, she followed me like an obedient little girl. "If you don't like herbal tea, how about some juice?" I asked.

"What kind?"

"Orange or prune," I offered.

"Prune!" she exclaimed. "Are you, like, a hundred years old, or what?"

"Orange it is." I smiled, choosing to ignore the hurtful comment that had hit a little too close to how I'd been feeling lately.

Once I'd poured her a small glass of juice, I wiped up the crumbs of my own toast, and then depositing two slices of fresh bread in the toaster for Geralyn.

When I turned back again, I caught her reaching across the table, intent on the half-filled cup of coffee I'd left behind.

"Geralyn! No," I said firmly.

"I want coffee!" she whined.

"Well, your baby doesn't! And, right now, you need to be thinking of him more than you're thinking of yourself."

"Well, I don't know why I have to," she protested. "I don't want this stupid kid anyway."

"Geralyn!" I exclaimed. "What a horrible thing to say."

"Well, I don't," she insisted.

I didn't know what to say. "Why don't you want the baby?" I

91

asked finally, sitting down across from her. "Have you discussed these feelings with Danny?"

"I can't discuss anything with Danny," she almost spat. "I could talk until the moon turns blue, and he wouldn't hear me."

"What do you mean?"

Geralyn grimaced, then turned away for a moment. When she turned back again, she looked at me defiantly.

"That's just what you wanted to hear, isn't it?" Her tone was accusing. "That he doesn't want to be with me? Well, he doesn't."

"Did he tell you that?" I asked.

"Yes," she admitted.

"When?"

"A month ago."

"A month ago?" I repeated. "A month ago, you were planning on getting married."

"Two wrongs don't make a right," she mimicked. It sounded as though she were repeating him verbatim.

She was silent for a moment. And, when she spoke again, her voice was filled with regret and resignation.

"I thought if I told him I was having his baby, he would change his mind about us. He might begin to see me in his future—instead of just his bed."

"Geralyn, is the baby Danny's?" I asked hesitantly.

"Yes!" she shouted before the words had entirely passed over my lips. "Of course, it's Danny's baby, Audra. What do you take me for?"

"Well, it's just the way you said it, I thought—"

"I know what you thought," she snapped.

"What are your plans?" I really wanted to know.

She looked at me long and hard, as if trying to decipher the hidden meaning in my question.

"I plan to go to work," she finally replied, but made no move to get up from the chair.

"You know what I mean." I was trying to remain calm, and keep a pleasant, patient tone to my voice. But what I really wanted to do was to shake her, and tell her to stop acting like the spoiled brat that I'd always known that she was!

"This baby's going to come into the world in a couple of months, whether you're ready or not," I reminded her.

"I should have had an abortion while I had the chance," she muttered.

It was just like Geralyn to say such a thing—for no better reason than the element of a good, strong shock.

"That certainly would have been an option at one time. But, not anymore. You're too far along," I said firmly.

"He offered me the money, you know," she continued. "That Prince Charming of yours. When I first told him that I was pregnant, almost the first words out of his mouth were to offer me money to go and have it done away with. He wanted me to kill the baby. He didn't want to let my perfect, wonderful sister know what a bad boy he really was!"

"Geralyn, please," I murmured.

"Please what, Audra? Please don't soil the image of your 'knight in shining armor?'" she asked sarcastically.

"That image was tarnished long before now, I assure you."

"Well, there was no way I was going to do that," she continued, as if I hadn't even spoken. "I wasn't going to let him sweep me away like that. I saw him first."

So that's what this is all about, I thought.

True to form, my little sister had been weighing her options and making her own selfish plans without a single thought for the future of the child that she'd created. It was all about weapons she could wield against me, to pay me back—revenge for falling in love. And, suddenly, there was yet another life caught in the crossfire. I sat there at that table staring at her, wishing for the millionth time that I'd never come back to Cold Harbor.

"If he doesn't marry me," she said coldly, "I swear I'll send this baby away when it's born. I'll put it up for adoption, and he'll never lay eyes on it."

And with that, Geralyn rose from the table and stalked out of the house. The slam of the door echoed for a long time after, and I remained frozen there like a stone statue.

I wasn't really sure of what led me down to the beach that afternoon. Some sort of strange magnetic pull seemed to be steering my car, until I'd found myself there on that old bench, staring out toward the water. I'd forgotten what a peaceful place it had been for me in days not so long past—days when Danny was always at my side.

After half an hour, maybe longer, I stood to stretch and nearly lost my footing.

"As graceful as ever," I heard someone say.

I turned to find Cecily standing there, and my immediate reaction was one of joy at seeing my old friend again. Until reality set in, and I remembered that I hadn't spoken to her since learning that she had kept Geralyn's secret along—just as everyone else I loved had done.

"What are you doing here?" I asked her, ignoring the disappointment in her eyes.

"I don't really know," she admitted, looking out over the water as if it were a long-lost friend. "I just needed to clear my head."

"Well, I won't interrupt," I told her.

I started back toward my car, but I hadn't gotten far when Cecily joined me, keeping up with me stride for stride.

"Audra, I've missed you so much. Will you talk to me?" she asked.

"I don't really have anything to say, Cecily," I said.

"Will you listen then?" she begged.

The truth was that I didn't feel like listening. I didn't feel like talking, or hashing over old hurts, or making polite conversation. I just wanted to be alone.

"How are things going at the house?" she asked, touching the sleeve of my jacket so softly that I might not have noticed.

"My sister and I weren't cut out to be roommates," I told her honestly. I sighed. "My mom is recovering and Geralyn is having Danny's baby. And I'm stuck back in this town, just the way I always feared I would be. And how are things with you, Cecily?"

My sarcasm had made Cecily blush uncomfortably.

"Is there anything I can say to fix things between us?" she asked.

After a moment's thought, I answered her the only way I could. "No," I replied honestly.

"I love you, Audra," she whispered.

"Funny," I nearly spat in reply. "So many people who supposedly love me, and yet—"

"Danny loves you, too," she told me.

I laughed bitterly.

"I made a mistake by not coming to you as soon as I'd heard about Geralyn's pregnancy," she went on. "I don't want to make that mistake again. But you don't make it easy to communicate with you, either."

"Cecily," I told her finally. "If you have something to say, just take a deep breath and spit it out, would you?"

"Danny is heartsick, Audra," she said.

"Oh, Cecily, please—" I began.

"He is—really. He's confided in Dave and—"

"I'm so happy to know that my ridiculous love life could be a bonding experience for your husband and the father of my sister's baby!"

"Geralyn has spoken to a lawyer, Audra. She's going to put the baby up for adoption without telling anyone. She wants to hurt Danny because she feels he's hurt her."

"How do you know that?" I asked cautiously.

"Dave plays softball with Walter Myers." She looked at me as if that one statement explained it all.

"And?" I had no idea of what that had to do with anything.

"Walter's wife, Joanne, works as a paralegal for Peter Wallingford.

He's the attorney who's handling the case."

My heart turned instantly stone cold. I had seen Peter Wallingford's business card on the kitchen counter only a week before.

"She's going to give up the baby the moment it's born. She wants to make sure that Danny will never even get to lay eyes on his own child."

It was just like Geralyn to plan something so heartless, and it broke my heart to realize that she was my sister.

"Danny's heart will break if that happens," I said aloud, as much to myself as to Cecily.

"He's not going to let that happen," she replied.

"He knows?" I asked.

She nodded. "Dave told him."

"What's he going to do?"

"Talk to him, Audra," she urged. "Lower that shield of anger and resentment, and just talk to him."

The thought drove a shard of glass straight into the most tender part of my chest.

"Are you finished?" I asked.

She didn't reply right away, and I took that as an opportunity.

"Good-bye, Cecily," I said as I got in my car and headed for home.

I didn't sleep well that night. I kept thinking of the look on Cecily's face as I'd peeled out of the parking lot and left her standing there. She'd been my best friend when we were growing up, and we'd barely ever exchanged a harsh word between us. But, learning that she had known the truth about Danny's affair with my younger sister had changed all of that, and I hadn't been able to think of her in those affectionate terms again since.

I blamed Cecily. And, I blamed Danny and Geralyn—and even my mother. I felt as though the whole town of Cold Harbor had formed some sort of bizarre alliance against me—a conspiracy of pain, betrayal, and blackmail—first to break my heart, and then, to force me into returning. My adult mind knew how childish it seemed, but the young girl who had escaped her life there was still alive and well inside of me, and she couldn't manage to let go of the tragic irony of it all.

And, I couldn't let go of the pain I felt for Danny, either. It must have been excruciating for him to discover what Geralyn had planned, and I couldn't help but to wonder what he was going to do. I couldn't let go of Cecily's words, either.

"Talk to him," she had said. The echo of those three words played again and again in my head until I could hardly stand the repetition. When Sunday morning finally dawned, I greeted it fully dressed and in my car, already on my way over to Danny's house.

"I can't believe it," he said when he opened the door to find me standing on his front porch.

"Can we talk?" I asked.

"Yes," he told me. I didn't think I'd ever seen anyone drown so quickly in a sea of relief.

"I can't believe that you're here," he murmured.

"Neither can I," I admitted.

"I'd stopped believing in miracles," he told me, and the emotion in his eyes scorched the edges of my heart until my eyes flooded with tears, too.

"It's Cecily's fault," I finally told him. "She told me that I had to talk to you, and I couldn't stop thinking about it."

"Well, thank goodness for Cecily," he said.

"That remains to be seen."

Danny and I were both silent for a long time that morning. Our gazes seemed to be welded together, and I heard every word that he didn't dare speak—so loud and clear that my ears rattled. What was worse, I knew that he could read my thoughts, too. The conversation was wordless, and yet so loud that it could have awakened the dead.

"I still love you," he said finally, and the silence shattered like glass around me.

"Please don't say that," I told him, but I didn't really mean it. Those were the words that I had been aching to hear for months.

"I love you," he repeated, then sat down on the sofa beside me and took me into his arms. I wanted to resist, but my body wouldn't follow and I collapsed into his embrace and began to sob.

"How could you?" I whispered.

"I don't know," he replied sincerely. "I've asked myself that question a thousand times. You'd left me, and I was lost. I made a mistake."

A mistake which had taken on a life all its own. A mistake that we couldn't repair—no matter how much we still felt for one another.

"Can you ever forgive me?" he asked.

I couldn't tell him that it was no longer a matter of forgiveness— that it had become an issue of much greater magnitude. How could we ever be together, after all that had happened? My heart and mind buzzed with questions, desperation, and despair.

"Because if you can tell me that you forgive me," he said, brushing the hair away from my face and drying the river of tears that was cascading silently down my cheeks with the back of his hand, "I can breathe again. And that will be the first step in finding the answer to this mess."

"There are no answers, Danny," I told him convincingly.

"Do you love me?" he asked softly.

I stared at him long and hard for a moment, and then, against my own better judgment, I nodded.

"You still love me," he whispered, his face filled with joy.

"But, after all that's happened," I pointed out, "love isn't going to be enough."

"It's the first step," he insisted, and then he pulled me close into him. "We're building something here, Audra. And it's going to be a slow process—one step at a time."

I wanted to believe him so badly that I was nearly pierced through with hope. Anything could happen from that moment on, I'd realized, but I'd also tasted hope one more time, faintly and yet distinctly, and I couldn't bear to let it go.

"I've told Geralyn that I'm not going to marry her," he explained, and it seemed like it was more to himself than to me. "We've made enough mistakes already. That would just be another."

"But, what about the baby?" I asked, and he silenced me with a soft kiss that was the answer to a silent question I'd been carrying around with me since the day we'd said good-bye.

"I'll take care of the baby," he said when we parted, still so close that I could taste his breath as it caressed my face. "Geralyn want to give the baby away when it's born."

"I know. Cecily told me," I murmured.

"I'm not going to let that happen," he stated firmly.

"How?" I asked.

"I've got an attorney working on that. But you can't tell her that you know anything. Or that I do, for that matter."

"I won't," I promised.

"I'll be a father to that baby," he told me seriously, holding my gaze to his with a fire I'd never seen in him before. "But I won't be a husband to any woman except you, Audra."

In no more than an instant, the moment became one of those that I'd read about in romance novels, and seen in the muted frames of wonderful, heart-stopping movies. There were no buttons or zippers or fumbling hands. There were only two spirits melting into one, like the wax of a candle on a fireplace mantle. I was a pitcher of warm liquid, and Danny poured me out and bathed himself in me until, three hours later, I awoke in his bed. And in his arms.

We made our plans that afternoon, the ones that would form the foundation for whatever would come for us. Declarations of love were fragile threads that surrounded us, binding us together in our quest, and we made promises to one another that day. Promises that shaped the windows of the new life that we were striving to create— promises through which I could almost see a horizon that glistened with possibilities that I'd once thought were dead.

97

I was nearly radiating when I walked through the door of my family home that evening. I was trying to be sensible, reasonable, and logical, but I was losing the battle. The afterglow of rekindled love burned in every fiber of my body, and I faced Geralyn with the fear that she could read it on me like a well-plotted novel.

"Where have you been all day?" she asked me casually.

In paradise, I thought, and then pressed hard on the words to keep them low in my heart.

"I had a million things to take care of," I commented.

"Well, I ordered a pizza for dinner," she said with a shrug. "There's some left over, if you want to heat it up."

"Thanks," I told her.

There was no more conversation to mar my feelings of utter bliss, and I was able to make my way upstairs for a warm bath—and the blessed solitude I craved—before any other questions were asked.

In the weeks that followed, Danny and I were cautious about our meetings, but each one was filled with excitement and a sort of fearless abandon which only found its wings behind the closed door of his bedroom late at night.

The doubts crept in occasionally, and I questioned myself about giving in to forgiveness without more of a fight. But then, I would look into Danny's eyes, and I would see the truth there. He was fighting with everything he had inside of him to make up for his substantial part in the mistakes that he'd made, and something new was being built in spite of them.

I provided as much support to Geralyn as I could in those days. I continued to prepare meals which contained enough nutrition for the growing child inside of her. I avoided talk of Danny, a subject she only touched upon occasionally, by encouraging her to think instead about the kind of mother she might want to be.

Things were easier once our own mother came home from rehab. She played the innocent, unknowing buffer between her two daughters, and provided enough of a distraction in her need for special care that there often wasn't time for much interaction between myself and Geralyn. I'd feel almost guilty at times for the part I was playing in the covert plans which would change my sister's life forever. But then, I'd extinguished the bouts of guilt and doubt with the knowledge that Danny and I really were meant to be, and that our plans were all a part of that destiny.

"Audra!" My sister's call pierced straight into my sleep and dragged me awake with white-hot clarity, and I rushed to Geralyn's room. From the doorway, I could see her perched at the edge of her bed, rocking back and forth.

"Geralyn?" I asked.

"Take me to the hospital," she pleaded. "It hurts."

"Is it time?"

"Yes, it's time," she snapped. "Get me to the car."

I helped my sister down the stairs. Then, I snatched up the overnight bag we'd packed the week before and placed it on the floor of the hall closet.

"Mom, I'll call you from the hospital," I called.

From the car, I used my cell phone to call Mrs. Walters and fill her in. We'd already arranged that she would go over to the house and stay with Mom when the moment arrived. And, indeed, it had arrived.

"Oh," Geralyn whispered. "This is horrible."

"Remember to do your breathing," I reminded her, punching in the number to Danny's pager as I soothed her. "Short, quick breaths."

And then, at the sound of the tone, I left the code we'd agreed upon. He would know what it meant.

"My sister is in labor," I announced to the nurse inside the emergency room door. "And the pains are coming very fast."

In hardly any time at all, Geralyn was where she needed to be, and the doctor told us that the baby would arrive in a very short while.

"So much for the old myth about first babies taking a long time," I joked, and Geralyn looked up at me in such a way that I almost began to cry. "Don't be scared," I reassured her. "You're going to be fine."

"Audra?" she began, then squeezed my hand so hard that I nearly doubled over.

"It's okay, Geralyn. Try to just breathe."

"This is torture," she told me.

"I know, honey. The doctor says that you're almost there."

The rush of activity that followed was incredible. Nurses flitted about, the doctor came, and a mask and gown were shoved into my hands. I barely had the mask tied at the back of my head before the baby had started to come, and I watched in the mirror as its little head arrived.

It was the most unbelievable sight I had ever beheld, and tears began to flow so quickly that I could hardly wipe them away fast enough to keep my eyes on the miracle before me. My heart raced with the knowledge that I was actually witnessing the dawn of life.

And not just any life. The baby was Danny's child. And, for better or worse, the child of my very own sister.

"It's a boy!" the doctor exclaimed just after Geralyn's final groan, and I looked on as the mucous was wiped away to reveal a tiny, squirming infant, still connected to my sister's body by the cord.

"Oh, Geralyn," I breathed, and I felt distinctly as if I might faint right there on the spot. "He's beautiful."

"Would you like to hold your son?" the doctor asked her, but Geralyn turned her head away in silence.

"Geralyn?" I asked.

"Take him away and leave me alone. I'm exhausted," she told the doctor.

The expressions of the medical team reflected my own, and I finally broke free and stepped over to Geralyn's side, wiping away the perspiration from her face.

"You did a good job," I told her softly, my heart quietly breaking inside my chest.

"It's over," she whispered, and then closed her eyes.

I found Danny in the waiting room, just as I'd known I would, and he got to his feet and embraced me as I approached him.

"You have a son," I told him.

"Already?" he asked incredulously.

I nodded. "A beautiful son."

We held hands as we peered through the glass of the nursery window, and then we both wept.

"My son," he said several times as we stood there. "I have a son."

I didn't get any sleep that night, despite the four hours I spent tossing and turning. All I could think about was what was about to happen.

I arrived at the hospital early that morning, but I couldn't pinpoint exactly why. I was filled with all sorts of hope. Hope that Geralyn would surprise us all, and hope that she wouldn't. But, my questions were answered within moments of entering her room on the maternity ward.

"What are you doing?" I asked.

Geralyn looked up at me, but only for a moment, before signing her name to the last page of a three-or four-page document. I recognized the man standing beside the bed as the attorney Cecily that had told me about.

"Geralyn?" I asked again.

"I'm signing the adoption papers," she stated almost defiantly.

"Geralyn, why?" I cried, but I already knew the answer to my own question. "He's your baby. Don't give him up just to spite Danny and me."

"I'm Peter Wallingford, your sister's attorney," the man said, extending his hand toward me. "I'll be assisting her in the adoption."

"Geralyn, please. Think this through," I begged.

"I warned you that this would happen," she said, narrowing her eyes with a sort of mixture of insolence and pride. "I warned Danny, too. If he doesn't want to marry the mother of his child—"

"You're willing never to see your own baby again just to get back at Danny for not following your lead into a loveless marriage?" I couldn't believe it.

"Yes."

That one syllable held all the weight of the world for me. I'd known what she was planning, and still, I'd hoped that she would come to her senses.

"She doesn't care about being a mother. She never did."

I turned to find Danny filling up the doorway, with shadows beneath his eyes as deep as if they'd been rubbed on with a smudge of charcoal.

"Did you call him?" Geralyn accused. "You had no right."

"He had a right, Geralyn. He has a right to meet his son."

"He's not your son!" she shouted, the shrill of her voice breaking with rage. "I've signed him away, and you can't stop it."

"This is the father?" Mr. Wallingford interjected. "And he didn't consent to the adoption?"

"Of course, I didn't consent," Danny spat. "I'd never consent to that."

"I was informed that you had given up your parental rights," the lawyer told him.

"The only thing I gave up was the idea of marrying his mother," Danny retorted. "And my attorney will be here momentarily to present you with a custody order, signed by a judge, granting me full custody of my son the moment he leaves this hospital."

"No!" Geralyn shouted, then grabbed at her stomach when the effort to fly from the bed proved agonizing. "You can't have my son."

"But you don't want him. You've just admitted to that in front of witnesses. We have several other witnesses who have signed affidavits stating that you've been planning to absolve your maternal rights for months now."

"I'll fight you, Danny. You won't have my son," she vowed.

Geralyn was wrong. The attorney Danny had hired was a good one, and a few days later, he was able to take his son home to the nursery he'd spent the last month preparing.

Aside from some pretty severe name-calling and a truckload of empty threats, Geralyn never spoke to me again after that. Within a few weeks of the birth, she'd packed up and moved away. And, a month later, Danny and I were married.

As I finish putting our story down on paper, I can look out the back window where my beautiful three-year-old stepson is building sand castles in the box next to the swing set. My mother is sitting in her wheelchair a few feet away, a glorious smile gracing her face as she watches her grandson. I never could have imagined such joy.

I worry about Geralyn often. About her fate, about her state of mind—and, about whether or not she'll drop back into our lives at some point and shatter the life that we've made. But on those nights when the fear gets the better of me, Danny holds me in his arms and reminds me of the impossible odds that we've already overcome.

"Nothing is impossible," he tells me. And the funny thing is that I believe him.

It's true that I never wanted to come back to Cold Harbor. It was a small town with small ideals and even smaller possibilities. Until Danny and I found our place within it. Now, you couldn't tear me away—not even if my life depended on it.

THE END

THE DEVIL WEARS STILETTOS
My Vixen Sister Made A Pact Of Sin. . . .

Tracks of black mascara ran down Lili's cheeks. Tangled hair brushed her bony shoulders. Her nose gave off an oily sheen and she wore a rumpled sweater. I plunked a box of Kleenex onto my kitchen table, poured her a cup of coffee, and urged her to sit right down.

Because my sister squanders several hours of every morning carefully styling her hair and meticulously applying makeup, I immediately sensed that something was out of whack.

Appreciative double takes and lusty leers cast in Lili's direction are elements that totally make her day. While I might sprint out to the mailbox wearing a flannel bathrobe, pink hair rollers, and my husband's rubber boots, my sister won't even deposit her garbage in the backyard can before she's fully decked out and groomed. And so, it didn't take more than a cursory glance at Lili's unkempt appearance to give me a clue that she was in the midst of a serious crisis.

Lili rocked her painted chair against my kitchen wall. "Jonah says he'll never get close to God if he's living with me!"

Now, that's not hard to figure, I contemplated. Living with Lili's like living with the devil himself. There isn't a man on earth who could get close to God if he kept company with my sister.

In typical Lili fashion, she'd baited me with a provocative comment concerning her most recent paramour. As it was, nothing would've made me happier than to probe her for further details, but I stuck to my sister's script and maintained a somber silence. Years of dealing with Lili's dramas have taught me not to ask questions until she's darn ready to give up the answers. In a well-rehearsed, but phony, effort to heighten my anticipation for her racy, romantic woes, Lili wailed and lamented as she noisily snuffled into a soggy Kleenex, and then flung it to the floor.

I watched her out of the corner of my eye as I pulled out the cutting board, reached for a knife, and commenced to dice up an onion and two green peppers. Feigning a lack of interest, but hoping for further enlightenment at the same time, I leaned over the stove, lifted a lid, and added the vegetables to a kettle of simmering broth. A three-by-five card thumb-tacked to my door reminds visitors to leave their smokes outside, but Lili struck a match with her thumbnail and lit a cigarette. The chicken soup bubbled over and I adjusted the flame under the burner and cocked the lid on the kettle.

"Can you imagine, Mary? Jonah just threw his clothes into a

103

cardboard box and walked out my front door without even looking back!" My sister tilted her head back, took a long drag on her cigarette, and looked calmer at once. "He didn't even give me a chance to pitch a fit!"

I raised my eyebrows, thinking, Now that's a crying shame!

Lili's angry outbursts are truly a sight to behold, but, because the potential for destruction and violence on such explosive occasions can be remarkable, first-time observers—unless they're exceptionally nimble—should outfit themselves in full body armor. Crockery and sharp kitchen implements sail across her ransacked rooms. Doors are slammed off of their hinges as words of uncommon usage sizzle from her tongue. Windows are shattered. Fisticuffs break out. Survivors consider themselves lucky to crawl away with blackened eyes, while the seriously maimed and injured are carted away in ambulances.

Yes—

My sister's rages can be highly . . . entertaining.

Only a fool wouldn't stick around to watch one.

"Well, Jonah isn't through with me yet!" Lili promised, crossing her heart—and hardening it at the same time. "After all, I've got one thing his church sure as heck can't give him! Mark my words, Mary—he'll be back before Sunday!"

My sister stuck out her lower lip, blew a stream of cigarette smoke toward the ceiling, and then dropped the butt into her cup of coffee. I gave the soup a stir and shook my head. Right then, there was no doubt in my mind that my sister would get what she set out for. I stepped over her long, skinny, outstretched legs and opened a window to air out the kitchen. My husband, Farley, can't abide the smell of smoke—

And he can smell a rat from a mile away.

The following Sunday I walked three doors down the road to Lili's house for a cup of coffee. Jonah answered my knock at the door wearing nothing but a threadbare towel. My cheeks burned instantly at the sight.

"Come on in, Mary; I'll show you my new tattoo."

I kept my eyes riveted to Jonah's forehead as the pink towel fastened at his waist slipped to his hips. The beyond-reform dude clearly wanted nothing more than to goad me, and a smile brightened his face with an almost—and I do mean, almost—saintly glow.

"That sister of yours! I'm backsliding again, Mary, but thank God for His forgiveness!"

The overpowering aroma of Jonah's cologne gave me a twinge of vertigo as he grabbed my trembling hand and pulled me inside. The towel slipped another inch and Jonah turned on a grin that would charm most women, but I never do trust any guy who's that good looking. I jerked my hand away and eased out the door just as Lili entered the room. She was dripping wet from her shower—

And naked as Paris Hilton.

Jonah may have had good intentions when he moved out of Lili's place, but I knew he didn't have a chance in heaven with a temptress like my sister lurking about. Oh—the man was backsliding, all right. As it was, the ground he stood on was so slippery that I knew he'd never gain a hold.

Lili played devil's advocate for the next three months. And even though Jonah never missed a Sunday service at the community church, she was still happier than a heathen. The Good Book says that love is a fire, and you can bet your sweet behind that Lili was keeping theirs stoked. She put those solitary Sunday mornings to good use, making sure that Jonah was not disappointed when he came calling after church. My husband, Farley, said that Lili probably bought bubble bath, perfume, and red nail polish by the ten-gallon drum.

But something wasn't right.

Why is Jonah keeping up the pretense of going to church if he's so bent on living a sinful life? I wondered. After puzzling over his intentions for a week, I finally resolved to leave off of my fretting. I figured his motives would come to light in the Lord's own time.

The manicured nail on Lili's index finger tapped out a rhythm on her grease-soaked menu. Sally's Diner serves up the best breakfast in three counties and my sister maintains that the fry cook who recently drifted into town is darn good looking, as well.

That day, she licked her lips with practiced seduction. By the way the guy at the grill was checking her out, you could tell the attraction was mutual—to say the least.

"I saw Jonah come out of the jewelry store yesterday morning," Lili matter-of-factly mentioned, never once taking her eyes off of the cook. "Wouldn't it be just like him to pop the question when I'm least expecting it? He knows I just love surprises!"

Well, you could've knocked me over with one of Lili's red feather boas when Jonah did tie the knot—the very next day.

But it wasn't my sister that he promised to love and cherish through good times and bad for the rest of his life.

While Lili was busily feathering their lusty love nest on Sunday mornings, a churchgoing gal named Megan captured Jonah's cheating heart.

Oh—you better believe that Lili threw the mother of all conniptions after she found out about that union! I would've given my right hand to see it! Kitchen chairs were reduced to splinters across her tabletop. A chandelier was shattered. Heirloom china bit the dust. You see, prior to Jonah, my sister always prided herself on being the partner who "called off" her frequent affairs. Jonah's the first time in her life that she didn't get her way. But even as hot tears flowed from her bedroom eyes, I knew that already, she was plotting her next move.

After all, my sister isn't exactly averse to breaking apart what God hath yoked together. She seduced her previous lover—a happily married man with two little girls—right out of her best friend's arms! Needless to say, Jonah and Megan didn't have a prayer once Lili mapped out her carnal course.

Rising up from the back pew of the community church, Lili minced down the aisle on four-inch, black stilettos as she came forward for the altar call the following Sunday. Her short, red dress was tighter than the skin on an apple.

The preacher laid his hands across her shoulders and commenced to pray. Lili might've convinced the congregation, but she didn't fool me one bit! The only reason why my sister "embraced" Jonah's religion was so that she could keep a pulse on him. Needless to say—

Lili didn't miss a single prayer meeting after that day.

If my next-door neighbor, Rachel, hadn't proven to be so reliable in relaying the details of my sister's shameful shenanigans, I honestly would've joined the church myself—just to keep abreast of the gossip! But I was spared that hypocritical deception; faithful, churchgoing woman that she is, Rachel beat a path to my back door minutes after the service let out at noon. I detected the telltale scritch of her nylon pantyhose scraping between her thighs as she squeezed through my hedge, scooted across the yard, and lumbered up my back steps.

"I'll tell it to you straight, Mary," Rachel clucked. "Jonah can't keep his eyes off Lili!" She dabbed powdered sugar off of her lips with a paper napkin even as the plump, sticky fingers on her free hand reached for a third doughnut from the white bakery bag. She dunked the maple-frosted confection into her cup of lukewarm coffee. "And that dress she was wearing today—if you can even call it a dress! You could've knocked my Jeff's eyes off with a stick!" Rachel took a deep breath as she shook her head and then licked the maple frosting from her fingers. "I sure feel sorry for Megan. That sweet girl's no match for Lili. Your sister could've given Jezebel a run for her money!"

As it turned out, Rachel's uncomplimentary observation proved to be prophetic.

Nobody questioned the paternity of the sweet baby boy Lili brought into this world not ten months after her "religious conversion." My sister's baby was born at six in the morning—while Megan gave birth to her firstborn son not three minutes later. Rachel—she's an obstetrics nurse—told me it's a toss-up as to who screamed the

106

loudest. And Jonah just about wore himself ragged running between the two birthing rooms.

I don't think I even have to tell you—after she pulled off that "crafty stunt," that's when I became convinced that my sister made a pact with the devil. There's no other way that those two births could have so curiously coincided.

For a week, my newborn nephew remained without a name. His mother bided her time, waiting to find out what Jonah and Megan would name their infant son. And then—Lili gave her little guy the very same name!

I never knew a person could be so wicked.

So that made two Zachary Jonah Grangers—both born on the very same day.

Twin sons from different mothers.

There oughta be a law!

Rachel refilled the sugar bowl with one hand and lifted the lid off of my cookie jar with the other. "I see it all the time in the profession I'm in, Mary." Her double chins jiggled when she shook her head. "Women who don't need babies have them, and those dying to have them can't."

Rachel's careless observation struck a touchy nerve. Instantly, my scalp tingled and blood rushed to my cheeks. Unmindful of my agitation, Rachel poked a snickerdoodle into her mouth. Cookie crumbs littered her spot at my table and she brushed them into her ample lap.

My neighbor knew, of course, about all of the trips that Farley and I made to the fertility clinic over the past seven years. No wonder I harbored a burning desire for Lili's baby to be Farley's and mine alone! Honestly, God forgive me, but I simply couldn't help thinking repeatedly: My spiteful sister gives birth to a child she doesn't even really want, while I'd give my right hand just to get pregnant!

It's the first time in my life that I was jealous of Lili.

Jonah continued to "drop in" on my sister whenever the passion struck, but alas—his heart clearly belonged to Megan. Tired of playing second fiddle, Lili schemed to tempt him back.

"If he won't leave his wife, then at least we can be neighbors," she announced one evening when I invited her over for lasagna.

And wouldn't you just know it?

The following day, a For Rent sign went up in the window of the rental beside Jonah and Megan's.

Always one to seize the moment, Lili packed up her belongings and slept in the house next door to her lover's that very same night. Less than fifty yards divided their bedroom windows, and you can bet that Lili propped hers open as a "neighborly welcoming gesture."

After that, it seemed like Jonah spent half of his time at my sister's place, "helping her out." If it wasn't "a drippy faucet," it was "a clogged drain." If it wasn't "a broken seal on the toilet," it was "a problem with the shower pressure."

"Good thing the man's a plumber," I told Farley. "I've never known a house to have so many leaky pipes!"

"Well, go figure, Mary. If Jonah earned his living as an electrician, your sister would find something haywire with the wiring, instead."

As it was, my husband strongly suspected that Lili was busting up her pipes with a monkey wrench just as quickly as Jonah could weld them back together.

Megan, of course, was fit to be tied. Lord knows, she did her best to keep the lovers at a distance, but the poor young woman simply never had a prayer.

The two mothers were neighbors for less than a month before Megan located another rental and moved her family to the other end of town. But wouldn't you know? Before Megan even unpacked their boxes, a For Rent sign appeared in the front window of the house next door!

That very afternoon, Lili paid the first and last month's rent on that little love nest and followed them again. The Lord only knows how she came up with all of that money—and on a bookkeeper's salary, no less!

"Looks like Jonah might have to re-plumb the whole house," Lili predicted when she dropped by my place later that week.

Why did it not surprise me that her new digs had even more plumbing woes than the previous rental?

"Jonah says he's never seen a house with such nasty pipes," Lili announced, applying a second coat of crimson polish to her nails, all the while smiling at her good fortune. "Do you s'pose you might watch the baby for me this afternoon, Mary? Jonah'll need my help fixing all those leaks."

I raised my eyebrows as I lifted little Zachary from his cradle and handed him to Lili. Receiving him with stiffened arms, she gave me a look that seemed to say, So? What do you expect me to do with this? The little tyke had yet to gladden his self-centered mother's heart. As it was, the less she had to deal with him, the better.

Indeed, it's true that, as it was, Zachary spent a good portion of his time in my care already. The handcrafted, cherry cradle that Farley made as a gift for Lili before her baby's birth had long since assumed a permanent position in our kitchen. Farley also bought her a stroller, a playpen, a car seat, and even a baby swing that plays lullabies when you wind it up.

Lucky for Lili, I'd quit my job at the cardboard box factory some weeks before. Such a move made me even more available and at the constant ready to help out the fledgling mother. Lili never really bonded with her baby, and so I wanted to make sure that I had plenty of time on my hands for any babysitting that she sent my way. Farley even bought me a rocking chair to keep in our big country kitchen, and to this day he swears I wore it out in a month, as much as I doted on that precious child. Not that he has any room to talk!

I never saw a man fuss over a baby like Farley did over little Zachary.

"I tell you, Mary, I sure could use some rest." Lili touched her slender fingers to her glossy mouth, closed her eyes, and yawned. "This baby's plumb wearing me out!"

I crossed my heart for thinking ill of Lili, but as often as she foisted that child off on me, she got more beauty rest than I ever did! Not that I cared even the tiniest bit, though! Little Zachary wasn't any trouble at all and I loved that tiny newborn every bit as much as I loved my own dear husband. As it was, Farley and I both looked forward to his daily visits—not to mention his ever-increasing overnight stays.

Oh, but the pride we felt whenever Zachary accompanied us on outings! Folks who didn't know us figured that he was our own little boy, and we just loved outfitting him in the manly little clothes that we searched for in various shops. And, of course—neither of us could ever resist buying him bright and colorful toys! Farley turned our living room into a regular tot's paradise before the little guy even learned how to crawl!

"He'll grow into it," I said, after buying Zachary the cutest, littlest, yellow raincoat in a size 3T two weeks after he was born.

"I know he's still too little, but he can just look at them, at least, for now," Farley said when he brought home a complete fleet of Tonka trucks when Zachary was barely six weeks old.

"Somebody's got to look out for the little fellow," we both justified, "seeing as how his own mama doesn't even keep diapers in stock."

"Hey. I'll probably be late tonight, Mary," Lili said, jolting me out of my reverie.

She plunked the baby onto my lap like he was nothing more than a ten-pound sack of spuds. Then, without even kissing little Zachary's peach-soft cheek good-bye, she finger-combed her hair with her one-inch nails and walked out my back door. If I knew my sister, she'd call within the hour, asking me to keep the baby overnight.

And how I wished with all of my heart that she would!

When she was gone, I just sat there in my kitchen rocking chair, stroking Zachary's downy, little head. The rocker creaked out a steady rhythm, a soothing lullaby that soon coaxed him back to sleep. His cheeks were flushed a healthy pink and five perfect, tiny fingers curled around my thumb. I bowed my head and breathed in his sweet, priceless baby smell as tears welled in my eyes.

Heaven help this child if he grows up with my sister, I thought as Zachary snuggled into my shoulder.

As if to agree, the baby breathed out a sleepy moan.

I was still rocking Zachary in my chair when Farley came home from work an hour later.

"Something tells me Lili's got another 'leaky pipe.' " He took a baby bottle out of the fridge and placed it in the warmer. "I'll bet you a nickel those 'pipes' won't get fixed tonight."

I gave my husband a hopeful smile, knowing full well that we were both more than happy to have Zachary spend the night in the canopied crib that Farley set up beside our bed. "I wouldn't be a bit surprised if Lili made up her bed this morning with red, satin sheets."

Farley leaned over the rocker and lifted Zachary from my arms. "Come here, little snort," he gruffly cooed as he gently flopped the baby over his lean shoulder and then softly stroked his rounded back. "This lady hasn't fed you your grub yet, has she, buddy?" He glanced toward the stove and hungrily sniffed the air. "Lazy woman hasn't even given a bit of thought to cooking my dinner, either!" he joked.

I lifted myself out of my rocker, sashayed over to the fridge, and pulled out a package of pork chops. After removing a knife from the rack, I proceeded to dice an onion. Farley gave my backside a pat with his free hand before he took my place in the rocking chair.

I turned around and grinned. Lord knows I would give that dear man anything he asked for if it were in my power.

As it was, it was always Farley's dream to have a son of his own—a wish that he never once mentioned again when we learned that I can't conceive. As it was, I cried every month when I got my period—a painful, cramping reminder that I'd failed him, once again. Farley would wipe the tears from my cheeks and hair, whispering over and over again that he didn't need a baby, just as long as he had me. Those words of comfort were music to my ears, even though I knew they were nothing but lies.

Maybe I'm more like my sister than I care to admit; after all, Lord knows I would've sold my soul to the devil for a son like Zachary. But until Satan made that tempting offer, I counted my blessings— such as the simple and painfully obvious fact that my sister was so disinterested in her own baby that almost all of his care fell to me—

And I thanked my lucky stars that she was "plagued with plumbing woes."

Another month passed. Megan located a cottage on the outskirts of town and the young family distanced themselves from my scheming sister once again.

I didn't even bat an eyelash when the house across the road from them came up for rent the very next day. By that time, there was absolutely no doubt in my mind regarding the fact that Lili had plainly struck up another deal with the devil, as she immediately plunked down her first and last month's deposits.

"Your sister should check with U-Haul about getting 'Frequent Mover Miles'," Farley groused as he hefted an unwieldy box up the sidewalk of Lili's latest digs. Then he plopped down wearily on the front steps.

On the other side of the road, Megan watched us from her porch. Even from that distance, I could see the fire in her eyes. She was rocking her own little Zachary Jonah Granger so fast that the chair had scooted across the porch and was fixing to rock right off of the edge. All at once, watching her, my heart went out to that poor woman as I thought, It's bad enough that her husband's heinously disloyal, but does he have to be so blatant, besides? Megan walked into her house with her baby in her arms and quietly closed the door as Farley and I lowered Lili's sofa from the moving van.

"Mind if I run a quick errand?" my sister had asked when we showed up to lend a hand with the packing earlier that day.

Without waiting for an answer, Lili pressed the baby into my arms, grabbed a monkey wrench, and hurried out the door.

"There're empty boxes in the bedroom if you need them," she tossed over her shoulder before roaring out of the driveway in her white Camaro. "And the keys to the new place are on the coffee table!"

My face reddened with irritation as I thought, That girl has more nerve than a spinal cord! Farley just rolled his eyes and kicked a packing crate. The pots and pans inside of it jangled.

"Well, at least she packed up the kitchen," I excused with a heavy sigh. "That's more than she did the last time."

We were both quick to make "allowances" for Lili. Call it "enabling," but the truth is—we would've done anything to get to spend more time with Zachary.

Lili never arrived home that evening to unpack the boxes that Farley and I stacked so neatly and orderly in each room. My sister didn't sleep in her bed that night—even though we made it up with freshly laundered sheets and blankets. No—

Lili vanished.

And Jonah was nowhere to be found, either.

When news of their "disappearance" made the circuit, nobody in our small town seemed even the least bit surprised by the very obvious fact that my sister left us minding her baby when she snuck out of town with her married lover.

Two weeks went by and Megan didn't even file a Missing Person Report on her errant husband—

But not a soul around faulted her for that.

In a town like ours, everybody knows your problems and everybody can see what's coming from miles away. It was just "a matter of time," everyone figured, before Jonah ultimately abandoned Megan—

And both Zachary Jonah Grangers.

So that's why you could've knocked every last one of us over with one of Lili's red feather boas when a hiker found Jonah's body at the bottom of an isolated ravine one month later.

The coroner reported that Jonah died instantly from a severe blow to the head.

Lili, of course, left no forwarding address.

It didn't take me long to figure everything out. Looking back, I see now that I should've seen the signs.

Even as a child, my sister refused to share her candy. The girl had a nasty temper from the moment of her birth, and I know darn well that she can wield a monkey wrench as well as any man.

She seemed guiltier, still, when the company where she worked reported an embezzlement of eighty thousand dollars.

Maybe it's a "pure coincidence" that the fry cook from Sally's Diner left town at the same time, but the reason for that is obvious to everyone, too. We all know Lili was carrying on with him on the nights when she wasn't carrying on with Jonah.

"Those sheriff's deputies think they're pretty smart, but they don't have a clue." I fanned myself with a newspaper as Rachel swirled the ice cubes in her glass of sweet tea. "I've read enough murder-mysteries over the years to figure the whole thing out."

My neighbor set down her glass on the picnic table and leaned forward expectantly on the bench. I purposefully ignored her. Yes—years of dealing with my sister taught me how to heighten the anticipation of grisly melodrama. So, although Rachel positively squirmed in her seat for more details, I bided my time—stretching out and prolonging her agony.

Zachary had nodded off to sleep on the baby blanket at my feet, his plump, little fist curled around the scoop shovel on one of his Tonka trucks. After gently loosening his fingers, I picked up the slumbering babe and rocked him on my chest. The branches of the honey locust tree in the middle of my backyard lifted with the late-afternoon breeze as Rachel inclined her head toward me, literally quivering with anticipation.

"It was a love triangle, all right—a bloody crime of passion. Correct me, Rachel, if I'm not right."

You see—

Lili knew that Jonah's heart was more inclined toward Megan's, and if my sister can't have a man completely, I figure she would just as soon see him dead. The only reason why Lili didn't kill Jonah sooner, I told Rachel, is because she lacked the funds to live in queenly style.

Making off with her employer's slush fund solved that quandary.

"I thought it was strange when Lili borrowed the English-to-Spanish dictionary I still had from high school the night before she vanished. But then I remembered: She's always had a real thirst for margaritas. And they say you can live pretty well in Mexico on fifteen dollars a day."

Rachel drained her glass of tea. She stood up and tugged her nurse's uniform down over her dimpled belly. "Well, I best get home, Mary—time to fix old Jeff's supper."

She cut across the back lawn, skirted the sandbox that Farley built when Zachary was two weeks old, and then squeezed through the gap in the hedges. From my position at the picnic table, I could hear the scritch of her pantyhose as she hightailed it across her yard.

It would've made me feel like a traitor to blow the whistle on my own flesh and blood. But I knew I could count on Rachel to spare me that trouble. As it was, I had a hunch that she'd call the county sheriff just as quickly as she could get to the phone—oh—not that law enforcement wasn't already hot on Lili's trail.

Gently flopping the sleeping baby over my shoulder and placing an arm across his back, I moved to the front porch glider to await the sheriff's arrival. A hot gust of wind blew the sweet scent of honeysuckle across my yard as the glider creaked out its steady, tranquilizing rhythm. I ran a finger across Zachary's downy, plump cheek and he opened his eyes and cooed at me like any adoring son. My heart fixing to burst, I hugged him to my chest.

Sheriff Leo arrived within ten minutes. He shortly convinced me that, "You can't protect a criminal—even if that criminal 'just happens' to be your own sister." He followed me into the house, down the dim hallway, and then into the back bedroom, where Farley stored Lili's packed-up possessions. I pointed out the stack of library books that Lili checked out before her disappearance—every last one of them about Mexico. A torn-out magazine ad marked the third chapter of a book on top of the pile. The brochure that it advertised promised to: teach the reader how to live like a king—or a queen—in Mexico on fifteen dollars a day.

"Your sister always did aspire to being a princess," Sheriff Leo unemotionally reflected. Like every other young guy in our town, he dated Lili back in high school—until she threw him over for a cuter guy. Leo flipped through the book and grimly shook his head. "You'll let me know, won't you, Mary, if you hear anything from Lili? Phone call, postcard, email, letter—anything at all. . . ."

Mexico's a big country.

I knew he didn't have the foggiest idea as to where to even begin looking for my sister.

"Not much I can do until then, I'm afraid, Mary—except collect these books as evidence," Leo sighed, lifting his shoulders in a gesture of weary resignation.

Let me tell you:

The whole time I was nodding my head—

I was wishing with my whole heart that I would never see Lili's face again—

Let alone get a postcard from her in the mail.

"Your baby sister's got herself in a mess of trouble, Mary," Leo told me. "And it's not just these overdue library books here."

Seeing as how we've been friends since childhood, he let me know "off the record" that Lili's fingerprints were on file from back when she was booked for possession of a controlled substance several years ago. As it was, he was still waiting to find out if the prints matched up with the ones found on the monkey wrench recovered near the scene of the crime. And then, of course, there was the embezzled eighty thousand dollars.

All fingers pointed to Lili.

"I'll clear up these library fines first thing in the morning," I told Leo, tears brimming in my eyes as I walked him to the door.

He offered me his handkerchief.

Yes, I sure must've looked a sorrowful sight, but those sniffles had nothing in the least to do with distress over a missing murderess. To be honest, they came from a wellspring of sweet relief and joy!

I hitched the baby up on my hip and then delicately ran a finger across his tender cheek. My heart fixing to burst, I hugged little Zachary to my chest.

Just then, the whistle blew from the warehouse at the south end of town. I knew then that Farley would be home in less than ten minutes—and that I'd given nary a thought to supper.

Lazy woman, indeed!

I laid Zachary on a quilt and surrounded him with toys to give him something colorful to reach for while I fried up some chicken breasts and started peeling potatoes for Farley's favorite potato salad.

Murder in a small town makes everyone nervous, so the sheriff wasted no time in completing his investigation. Lili's fingerprints matched the ones found on the monkey wrench that was buried fifty yards from Jonah's body. Leo gave me a full report the following afternoon to spare me the shock of hearing it through the grapevine:

My sister was wanted for murder.

But a year went by, and Lili remained at large. Personally, right from the get-go, I knew deep down in my gut that unless she turned into an absolute fool overnight, my baby sister would find herself a sleepy, little Mexican village to settle down in and never again set her course in a northerly direction. Through the years, my sister's been branded with many a name, but nobody's ever called her a fool. No— right from the get-go, something told me that little Zachary would never again set eyes on his mother.

But I was wrong about that.

One year and two months later, Lili was arrested for drug trafficking in a Texas border town, and then extradited back to our state. The murder trial that soon followed garnered little attention outside of our county, but the brutality and senselessness of the crime compelled the jury to sentence my sister to life in prison without the possibility of parole.

Zachary is six years old today, and he calls me "Momma Mary." You never saw a nicer child.

The other Zachary Jonah Granger is a wonderful, precious little boy, too. I'm Aunt Mary to him.

Megan and I are throwing them a joint birthday party as soon as school lets out. Farley got off from work early today to help me blow up the balloons and twist the streamers. Rachel baked two devil's food cakes, and it will be all that we can do to keep her fingers out of the frosting until the little guests arrive. Sheriff Leo promised to cruise by "so all those little hoodlums can blast my siren." The truth is—he's dating Megan. No doubt they'll be married within six months.

Lord, how time flies! It seems like only yesterday that the county judge awarded custody of little Zachary to Farley and me. And what a happy day that was! The whole neighborhood turned out to celebrate our good fortune. They gave us a baby shower, too, even though the little tyke was almost three years old by then!

Farley and I never were churchgoers, but we went forward for the altar call at the community church the following Sunday. There wasn't a dry eye in the entire congregation when the preacher placed his hands on our shoulders and commenced to pray.

Yes—I am firmly convinced that the Lord works in mysterious ways.

I didn't even have to sell my soul to the devil to receive my reward.

THE END

SISTERLY LOVE
We both want the same man

"Look, Maggie, you've got to do this small favor for me."

"Small? I think not."

"It's only a few hours of your life. Besides, you'll be getting a free meal."

"Great, Michelle, but what you're asking me to do is wrong."

"Who'll know besides us?"

"That's not the point. What if I make a mistake?"

"Kevin will never know. I've only gone out with him once. If he wasn't such a sweet guy, I'd stand him up."

"Why can't you be happy dating one guy at a time, like most women?"

"Tie myself down to only one man when there are so many out there? You've got to be kidding."

I shook my head in wonderment at her callous attitude. Michelle was my identical twin. It was difficult to tell us apart physically, but that's where the similarity ended. I, for one, had quite the opposite outlook on dating. I could hardly date more than one guy at a time. I would be the one to mix up their names. Suddenly, I realized that Michelle was talking to me.

"So, sis, are you going to help me out here or not?"

"I don't know." I loved my sister, but I hated getting mixed up in her hair-brained schemes. I could go out with Kevin since I didn't have a date already lined up for the evening, but I still had a great many reservations. "Okay, but don't ask me to do something like this again. And if he expects to come in for a nightcap—"

"Maggie, he won't. He's a gentleman. Trust me."

Oh, had I heard those words before. "Okay, give me all the particulars."

Michelle told me everything I'd need to know—or the little she really knew about Kevin Moore. She was very strict about her screening process. On their first date, Kevin met Michelle at a fancy restaurant. From there they went on a quiet, moon-lit walk. He didn't sound like the usual type of guy that she dated. Michelle lived for the thrills. She was a spur-of-the-moment type of girl who loved fast cars and the men who drove them. Her impulsiveness ruled her life, often causing her to spend half of her time undoing the damage she'd done. As a child, I envied her. As an adult, I realized that I needed more order and calm in my life.

116

As we parted, she addressed the look of apprehension etched across my face. "I give you my word that after this one time I'll never ask you to take my place again. I intend to buy a planner to keep my scheduling straight." She laughed and waved as she began to walk away.

"Wait a minute," I called to her. "Where should he pick me up? At your place or mine?"

"Good question," Michelle said. "I was supposed to call him today to give him my address so he could pick me up. I guess when I call I'll just give him your address. That way you won't have to rush over to my place and you can spend more time getting ready."

I went back to my apartment to get ready for the date. I chose something daring to wear. That would be more in character with Michelle. It was a tight-fitting red dress. I'd bought it during a fleeting moment of weakness and had never worn it. As I studied myself in the mirror, I thought that I just might pull the ruse off.

Kevin came to my apartment at eight o'clock sharp. He was punctual. I liked that in a person, since I was always on time myself.

He'd told Michelle that he'd be taking her to a restaurant with a dance floor. I loved to dance and looked forward to it.

I didn't expect Kevin to be so handsome. When Michelle kept emphasizing how nice he was, I thought she was trying to compensate for his lack of good looks. Was I ever wrong!

"Ready to go, Michelle?"

I nearly corrected him and uttered my real name. Michelle would have killed me. I nodded, really afraid to open my mouth. He held the door open for me and led me to his car.

"You look great," he said.

"Thank you," I replied, thinking to myself: So far so good. But can I keep up the charade for an entire evening?

"You seem unusually quiet tonight."

I had forgotten that Michelle could be quite the talker.

"Just on my best behavior."

Kevin chuckled. I liked the sound of his laugh; it was warm and rich.

We drove to a restaurant on the outskirts of town. I nearly gasped when I first saw it.

"I know it isn't much to look at from the outside, but trust me, you'll love the place."

I gave him a reassuring smile. He seemed to appreciate it, and gave my hand a gentle pat. We parked and he held the car door open for me. Then, taking my hand in his, he led me inside. I could feel the warm atmosphere of the place envelop us as the maitre d' led us to a little table in a corner. A band was playing a smooth jazz tune while a few couples were on the dance floor, moving to the beat.

We ordered our meals and then joined the other couples on the dance floor. It was a slow dance, and I floated into Kevin's arms. He drew me close.

"Did I mention how nice you look tonight?" he asked.

"I think you did."

"You deserve to be told again and again."

"Why, thank you. You know, you look quite handsome yourself."

"Now you know why I said that."

I broke into laughter and playfully punched his shoulder. "Is this some kind of new spin on 'I'll scratch your back if you'll scratch mine?'"

"No, but we can do that later."

"Now that's what I call wishful thinking," I said with a laugh.

Before long, we were both laughing. I felt so comfortable being with him. Then I remembered I was supposed to be standing in for Michelle. By the time the band finished the song, I knew I wanted this man and hated the fact that I'd have to let him go.

The next song was a fast one. Kevin was a good dancer. People around us stopped to watch. Normally I'd be very self-conscious, but dancing with Kevin and enjoying myself so, I wasn't. By the time the song had ended, we were both out of breath and needed to sit down.

"Where did you learn to dance like that?" I asked.

"My aunt worked in a dancing school and needed a partner to practice with."

The waiter brought us our salads. I watched Kevin as he ate and wondered why my sister was interested in him, aside from his obvious good looks. They were such opposites. He was clearly more conservative and reserved than her. I didn't detect any impulsiveness on his part. My sister was daring. She liked to walk on the wild side, always a part of the cutting edge of things. Kevin was definitely more my type.

I finally began to put together all the fragmented bits of thought that had been floating around in the back of my mind since the night began. I wanted Kevin for myself. I wanted to continue to date him. Thinking about it was easy. Telling my charming sister wouldn't be. She'd skin me alive before allowing me to take a man from her. Knowing this, there would be little future for Kevin and me. Unless Michelle didn't know.

Then the solution came to me. All I had to do was tell Michelle that the date didn't work out and Kevin didn't ask for another. These things did happen—even to my sister. Then I had to keep the three of us apart, until I had made Kevin completely mine. After that, what my sister thought or did wouldn't matter. Of course, by then Kevin would know I was really Maggie. The plan sounded simple enough.

By the time Kevin and I had danced most of the night away, I knew I had made the right decision. There was no way that I was going to allow Michelle to take him from me. It was so easy for her to meet guys and sweep them off their feet. I never found dating that simple. With Kevin so attainable, I wanted to hold on to him with all my might.

We left the restaurant laughing. I couldn't remember the last time I felt so comfortable with a man. It was as if I'd known Kevin for years. It certainly didn't feel like a first date.

I was so wrapped up in the euphoria being with Kevin had draped around me that I did something I'd never do on a normal first date. I asked him if he wanted to come back to my place for a nightcap.

"I'd like that very much," he replied, grinning.

I then realized how relieved I was that he said yes. "It just seems too early to let the night end."

"I'm glad you're having a good time. If you're free, we can get together again next Saturday."

"I'll clear my social calendar," I said, trying not to grin like an idiot.

"That's a good sign," he said as he gazed deeply into my eyes.

A moment later, he drew me close and kissed me. I felt an instant surge of electricity course right through me. Who needed bells?

When we got back to my apartment, I told him to make himself at home while I got the wine. I found him tinkering with the piano in the living room.

"Do you play?" I asked.

"My mother forced me to take lessons when I was a kid. I still remember a little. And you?"

"Sounds like you remember a great deal. In my family, it was my father who made us take lessons."

I handed him his glass of wine. We sat down together on the bench and began to play a duet. On the second round, Kevin began to improvise a jazz riff as I continued the original refrain. This led to a unique rendition of "Chopsticks" before we ended in laughter. As the night wore on, I discovered so many things we had in common. I began to wonder what else we had in common, and I looked forward to finding out.

"You make me feel good, Michelle."

"I'm glad. You're a nice guy, Kevin."

I saw that look in his eyes again and hoped he'd kiss me. I got my wish as he took my glass and put it down next to his. His lips were soft and inviting. One kiss led to another, and before long I realized that I didn't want him to leave.

Suddenly, feeling wanton, I took his hand and led him into the bedroom. I didn't care what he thought. I wanted to show him how I felt.

"Are you certain?" he asked.

"Never so certain before."

He answered me with a kiss, and we loved the rest of the night away.

The next day, waking in Kevin's strong arms, I felt no guilt, just bliss. I had totally forgotten about Michelle—until he called me by her name. Then reality set in and I knew that I'd have to call my sister sometime.

Kevin and I had a late breakfast and went for a leisurely ride, then we had an early dinner at a quiet little restaurant.

"I really enjoyed this weekend, Kevin."

"I did, too. It's difficult to find people who enjoy similar things."

"I'll be looking forward to next Saturday."

"So will I. If you don't mind giving me your phone number, I'll call you during the week," he said.

I debated giving him Michelle's number for an instant before writing down my own. Satisfied with my decision, I smiled and handed him the slip of paper.

Glancing at his watch, he said, "We should start back now."

We got back to my place around seven-thirty and said our good-byes. I truly missed him as he drove away. The ringing of the telephone changed my mood, though, for I guessed who it would be.

"Where in the world have you been?" my sister inquired.

"No place special," I lied.

"So when are you—I mean, me, of course—going out with Kevin again?"

"You're not." But I am, I thought to myself.

"What?"

"The date turned out to be a bust."

"What's that supposed to mean?"

"Exactly as it sounds."

"You screwed up, didn't you?"

"No, I did not. I played you perfectly. Kevin turned out to be a winner, that's all."

"You were turned off by his advances, weren't you? When are you going to loosen up and have some fun in your life?" Michelle asked.

"It never got that far." Suddenly a delightful flashback of myself surrendering to Kevin's kisses stirred my senses. My sister would never know how wrong she was about me. "How many times did you actually go out with Kevin?"

"Once. Why?"

"Do you always expect men to make advances on the second date?"

"Well, usually, I guess."

"Well, the men whom I date sometimes don't make advances until the third date or later."

"You date nerds."

"Is that what you call nice guys?"

"Okay, you made your point. So what went wrong with the date?"

"He was too nice."

"I don't follow."

I began to let this fabrication take on a life of its own. "He's not our type."

"What's wrong with Kevin?"

"I got the feeling that he may be gay." I couldn't stop the lies once they started.

"You're kidding? That's not the first impression I got from him."

"First impressions are often deceiving. You've got to open a book to read it."

"I guess I wasn't looking beyond his good looks."

"I guess not. No loss. I'll live. The food at the restaurant was good, though."

"Look, thanks anyway for helping me out, Maggie."

"No problem. Oh, by the way, how did your date work out?"

"I'm seeing him Saturday night."

"Way to go, sis." At least she'd have another guy to occupy her thoughts. I felt less guilty about what I'd done.

Kevin called the next night. I was glad to hear from him. After all, all my free thoughts seemed to be about him. I hoped he thought of me as much. We made plans for Saturday night.

The week flew by, and soon I was with Kevin again. We saw a movie and had a late dinner. The weekend became nearly a carbon copy of the preceding one. I knew by then that I had fallen in love with this man.

We continued to date, and sometimes I met him for lunch during the week. Before I realized it, we had been seeing one another for over three months. I knew he cared for me as well, especially when he took me home to meet his parents.

I'd been nervous about this dinner, but he reassured me that his parents were very down-to-earth people and would love me. His married sister and her family would be there as well, and that added to my nerves. However, all my fears were for naught because I had a terrific time. They wanted to like me and were happy for Kevin. His sister, Rachel, told me why.

I was in the kitchen with her, helping her make the coffee when she told me about Kevin's last girlfriend, Vanessa. "They went out for over a year," Rachel explained. "Kevin wanted to marry her and thought she felt the same way about him. He wanted to surprise her with a ring and asked me to help him pick one. I never saw him so happy. The night he went to her apartment with the ring to propose to her, he found her in bed with another man. It devastated him."

"That's unbelievable. What did she have to say for herself?"

"Nothing. He didn't stay around for an explanation. Believe it or not, you're the first girl he's let get close to him since then."

"I love your brother and would never cheat on him."

She looked at me for a moment before replying, "No, I don't think you would."

The opening of the kitchen door interrupted our conversation. Kevin stuck his head in and asked if we were still alive.

"A little patience goes a long way, mister," Rachel replied. "We're just about finished."

"Just keep in mind that it is cruel and unjust punishment to withhold dessert from a guy."

"Go sit down!" Rachel ordered, and Kevin obeyed. We cracked up laughing. She was still his big sister.

On the way home, Kevin said, "You and my sister certainly had a long talk."

"Yes, we did. You have a lovely family."

"I guess I do. Sometimes I may take my sister for granted, but no matter what, she's always been there for me."

"I wish that I was as fortunate. Sometimes I think my sister cares too much about herself and too little about others."

Time had continued to slip away, and I still hadn't found the right moment to tell Kevin what I had done for my sister. This meant that he was still calling me Michelle. After hearing how his former girlfriend hurt him, I feared his reaction. I realized that the truth would probably set me free, but I was afraid Kevin might, too. I didn't want to lose him. I was a coward and certainly unprepared for his reaction when Michelle saw us at the mall together. He didn't know that my sister was an identical twin.

It was a freak meeting. One Saturday morning the buckle on Kevin's favorite belt broke. To console him, I suggested we go to the mall and try to find a new one that was similar. Michelle spied us walking into a men's store. She called my name, and I was able to stop myself from turning around. I tried to make believe that I hadn't heard her, but knowing my sister, I should have realized that she'd be persistent—especially after she saw me with Kevin. She didn't have to be a scholar to figure out that I had lied to her. When she finally caught up with us, I could see that she was furious.

"How could you, Maggie?" she yelled.

Kevin was rooted to the ground in shock. He looked from Michelle to me and back again. "She called you Maggie. Is that your name?" he asked me.

"It sure is. I'm the real Michelle," my sister spat at him.

"What's going on?"

"She never told you?"

Kevin glared at Michelle, silently asking her to get to the point.

"I asked my loving sister to keep a date I had with you because I couldn't. Some favor! She steals you from me."

"Is what she's saying true?"

"Yes, but Michelle fails to emphasize how I didn't want to deceive you in the first place," I hedged.

"I don't believe any of this." Kevin threw his hands up in the air.

"I went on the date with you to help her out, but I never expected to fall in love with you."

"Are you sure it wasn't more like, gee, my sister has so many guys, she won't miss one. Can't you even get your own guys?" Michelle cut in.

"So our entire relationship is based on a lie?" Kevin asked.

I shook my head, but Michelle bellowed, "It sure is. Give that rocket scientist a Nobel Prize!"

Kevin glared at her and grabbed my hand. "We're out of here. I'm taking you home," he said.

I could feel Michelle's eyes boring holes in my back. Certainly if looks could kill, I'd be lying on the ground dead. The tears that had been welling in my eyes began to slip down my cheeks. Selfishly my anguish concerned losing Kevin, rather than hurting my sister. Kevin remained mute the entire drive back to my apartment. He refused to discuss the matter with me and merely stared straight ahead as he drove. I feared that I had lost him for good. By the time he pulled up in front of my place and said good-bye, I was positive he wanted nothing to do with me.

Reluctantly I opened the car door and walked away. As Kevin sped off, he took my heart and soul with him. I didn't think I'd ever be whole again.

Michelle called later that night and made me even more miserable. If that was her intent, she did a great job. I ended up hanging up on her. After that awful phone call, I crawled into bed and cried myself to sleep.

When I opened my eyes the following day, I felt worse and didn't bother getting out of bed. I'd hoped that Kevin would call, but he didn't. Every time I closed my eyes, he was there. My every thought concerned him. How was I going to get on with my life without him?

I guess when you're down, everything goes awry. I lost a really big client. It was mostly due to the economy and not my own actions that caused this, but it still looked bad for me. The people living in the apartment above me had a leak in their bathroom. I came home to find the water streaming down through the ceiling, adding to the half inch of water that had already fallen. I put buckets down and tried to mop up what I could. Then I called the landlord, who assured me that everything would be taken care of as soon as possible.

Ironically, nothing could compare to the pain I felt in losing Kevin.

I missed his warm smile and exciting touch. My mind's eye kept replaying the events of the day we ran into Michelle at the mall. I kept seeing the terrible, hurt expression on his face that soon turned into anger. For me it was like pouring salt on a never-healing wound. I knew Kevin would find out about our ruse eventually. I just never thought he'd react the way he did. I wished I could go back in time and redo everything.

An entire week had gone by and I still felt as miserable as I did when it all happened. Whoever said that time heals all wounds?

I dreaded the start of another week. I couldn't wait to see what new things were coming my way. My supervisor sensed something was wrong and called me into his office to have a little chat.

He thought I was just tired and needed some recharging. His solution was a nice vacation. Unfortunately, having too much free time on my hands would be more detrimental to my health, because I'd have more time to think about Kevin. I tried very hard to convince my boss that I'd be my snappy self on Monday morning, after I rested up over the weekend. Whether he bought my line was another story.

After putting on a show for all my associates, I left Monday evening feeling exhausted. Play-acting really wasn't my bag. All I wanted to do was soak in a nice, hot bath until I turned into a living prune. Then I remembered that I had to wash a ton of towels and dry them before I was able to do just that. I had used them mopping up my bathroom. The good part was that the management had fixed the leak in the upstairs apartment.

I parked the car and began to walk toward my door. At first I thought that my mind was playing tricks on me, but it wasn't an apparition. Kevin was leaning against the railing, waiting for me.

"Kevin?" I said as I began to run toward him.

He placed a finger against my lips. Then, pulling me toward him, he kissed me. It began as a tender kiss, but soon it intensified to a feverish pitch. I could feel tears of joy streaming down my face. When we parted, he gently wiped them away.

"I missed you," he whispered, holding me in his arms once more. "I had no idea what a major part of my life you'd become."

"I missed you, too."

"I reacted like an idiot. Who cares how we met or what you call yourself? It's who you are that counts. I love you, Maggie."

"I thought I'd never see you again."

"I promise you that I'll never let you go. Not now, not ever," he said, sealing his vow with a kiss.

THE END

A STAND-IN FOR LOVE
I Took My Sister's Place At The Altar

I found the note lying on her pillow on a Saturday morning. The message was vintage Charlene.

I've gone on a much-needed vacation. Can't take the stress any more. Tell Mason the wedding is off.

As usual, she'd left a mess for someone else to deal with. I'd give ten to one odds her vacation plans had included the handsome trust fund lawyer she'd met last weekend in a local bar.

"Jill, where's your sister?" my mother asked, eyeing the note in my hand, a fragrant cup of coffee in hers. "Breakfast is ready."

"She's gone."

I held out the note.

Mom read the succinct message, her eyes widening.

"You're supposed to tell Mason the wedding is off?"

"Looks that way."

But I'd leave out my suspicions that Charlene hadn't left alone. How else could she afford a vacation—except on someone else's dime? She'd quit her job weeks before, claiming she was overburdened with wedding plans. Funny thing about that: I could have sworn I was the one doing all the legwork and phone calls, while she shopped for the perfect dress.

"No. That's not fair. I'll tell him."

"It's okay, Mom. Really. Mason and I are friends. I'll do it."

"This is going too far: leaving you to deal with telling her fiancé and canceling all the wedding plans." Mom said with firm resolve. "Lord knows how much money we'll lose on deposits!"

An unspoken secret hovered between us. It wasn't the money Mom was really upset about. I had to tell my long-time friend—the man I loved—that my sister had jilted him.

Mason made it easy. He showed up at the house about an hour after breakfast—a serious expression on his handsome face.

"Hey," he said in greeting. "I need to speak to Charlene—if she's up."

My heart sank as I let him in and broke the news. I waited, hands clasped in front of me, when he simply sat down on the sofa, shook his head, and smiled.

"Mason? Are you okay?"

I sat next to him, needing to touch him, the dark hair on his arms rough under my fingers.

The news obviously hadn't sunk in, or maybe he was in shock.

"Yeah. I'm great. Charlene just saved me from a break-up scene I was sure would be messy and hateful."

I searched his gaze, and found nothing but relief etched on his face.

"You came here to call off the wedding?"

The idea didn't jibe with the man who'd patiently helped me make decisions regarding their nuptials whenever Charlene deemed them too trivial for her to notice.

"Yes, I was. I've felt unsettled about my relationship with Charlene for weeks now, and the truth is. . . ." Mason paused, then turned his startlingly blue eyes on me. "I've discovered I'm in love with someone else."

"Oh." I jerked my hand back. It seemed as if I were the one devastated. I wanted to disappear.

During all the wedding preparations, I hadn't allowed myself to dwell on what could never be—hiding my true feelings from everyone except a mother who knew me too well. But in those few stunned moments after reading my sister's note, a guilty kernel of hope had planted itself in my heart.

"Jill, I—"

"You don't owe me any explanations," I interrupted, afraid I'd run screaming out of the room if I had to sit and hear how another woman had captured Mason's heart. "It obviously wasn't meant to be. I'm just glad you guys came to your senses before it was too late. Now, if you'll excuse me, I have an appointment across town."

I stood, and Mason did the same.

"Don't worry about canceling anything right now, Jill. We'll talk about that next week."

"Right."

Not if I had anything to do with it. I was staying as far away from Mason as I could get. We could handle the cancellations by phone. Someday, I would get over him. Until then, there was no need to torture myself with what might have been.

After a good cry in the privacy of my bedroom, I got back to the business of living. Grocery shopping, cleaning, laundry, church on Sunday, and back to work the next day kept me busy—but not enough. Memories of Mason surfaced at odd times: jokes we'd laughed over, political topics we'd debated with fervor, and a special moment for me—when we'd danced at his and Charlene's engagement party. There, within his embrace, he'd looked at me with admiration shining in his eyes, and said I'd become a special woman any man would be lucky to have.

Any man other than him, apparently.

Even that knowledge hadn't kept me from dreaming that it was he and I picking out the various accessories for the wedding, us in the secluded little honeymoon bungalow in Jamaica. I'd even gone so far as to wonder what our children would look like.

I avoided Mason's calls, leaving replies on his machine when I knew he would be out. In the wee hours of the morning, I'd wake up crying.

Three days later, I came home from a long day at the office to find Mason waiting for me in a quiet house.

"How'd you get in?" I asked.

"Your mom let me in before she left for her aerobics class."

The air in the room felt electrically charged, and I stared at him. Something was different, today. It wasn't the jeans and baby blue T-shirt that complemented his eyes and dark hair perfectly, nor the recent hair cut. But what I saw in his gaze kicked my pulse into overdrive.

Excitement, uncertainty and . . . interest?

I moved toward the hallway—afraid I'd become delusional from lack of sleep.

"Jill, wait—"

"Just give me a minute to change, and I'll be right with you."

My eyes must be playing tricks on me. Mason didn't look at me like that—ever. Why would he do so now, when he'd said he was in love with someone else? I considered myself passably pretty and kept in shape, but didn't kid myself about ever having the flashy, voluptuous beauty God gave Charlene. Guys didn't go from caviar and champagne to meatloaf and potatoes. He must be here to tell me about his new love, I thought.

Closing my eyes, I rested my forehead against the cool wood framing my bedroom door, took a deep breath, and let it out slowly. Damn. This was going to be hard.

"Jill?" Mason's voice came from directly behind my left ear.

I whirled around with a gasp.

"Wha—"

His hand clamped across my lips.

"Just listen. Then, if you want me to leave, I will."

I nodded.

"This was so not how I pictured telling you, but—" He dipped his head for a moment, then looked right at me. "I love you. No one else. Just you. I don't know how or why it happened, but it did. When we were making wedding plans, I found myself wishing there were more decisions to be made, more time we could spend together. But when I pictured you walking down that aisle toward me—that's when I knew. You were the one I was supposed to be with. Only you."

Somewhere in his nervous speech, I relaxed against the wall behind me, my off-kilter world finally righting itself.

Mason slowly removed his hand. His gaze worried me now that he'd stopped talking.

My throat tightened with emotion. I couldn't speak.

"Oh, God. Please tell me you'll give us a chance. I swear I'll prove it—"

I joined my lips to his, telling him everything was more than okay in the only way I could at the moment. There are no words to adequately express what I felt, so I poured my response into that kiss.

After an eternity, we eased apart.

"Does this mean?"

Mason stopped, as if afraid to ask the question.

"That I love you? Yes!"

His arms closed around me, lifting me off the floor, and I began to laugh.

"What's so funny?" he asked, lowering me until my feet touched down.

"Us. Making wedding plans that'll never happen, seeing ourselves in that church—together."

"It seems a shame to cancel what was going to be a great beginning. Would it be—" Mason broke off, with a shake of his head. "Never mind. I guess that would be too weird, right?"

Turns out, it didn't feel weird at all. The choices for the wedding had been ours—together.

That weekend, Mason surprised me with a beautiful diamond solitaire, a romantic dinner, and a formal proposal. At our wedding three months later, if anyone thought it was strange to see the bride's sister taking her place, no one said so. I'd like to think it was the love shining in Mason's eyes that told our guests his substitute bride was the choice of his heart.

THE END

I'M KILLING MY
OWN SISTER

My sister was dying, and it was all my fault. Just thinking about that made me want to hurl. I sat on my comforter and hugged my knees against my chest. I hadn't bothered to pull off my brand-name tennis shoes as dirt streaks smeared across my bed. Mom would have a screaming fit when she saw the mess, but I hadn't cared.

Nothing mattered anymore. Tears streamed down my cheeks and soaked into the knees of my jeans.

I set my whole family on this road to agony, I thought. And over nothing.

Lauren might die. And my own hateful words had caused her to be sick.

I didn't mean to make my sister sick. I didn't even mean to hurt her. I was just mad because she wouldn't let me borrow her new cashmere sweater, and she was really mean about it. I even asked her twice, as nicely as I knew how.

"Please, Lauren," I begged. "I won't spill anything on it —I promise. The green and amber makes my eyes look really good. Let me wear it just this once. It's important."

"No, Megan, you'll sweat it up. I'm saving it for Friday. I think that Kenny Wilson is going to ask me to the movies."

"I won't sweat, I swear. And if I do, I'll wash the sweater out right after school."

"It wouldn't be the same. It would be used. I want it to be brand-new for Friday."

Lauren added another coat of a new fingernail polish called Guava Stain to her nails—the same color that all of the popular girls at school were wearing. I thought that particular color was ugly, but I kept that to myself. I knew darned well that if it weren't for Lauren, the kids at school would call me a geek. But since I was the sister of a popular cheerleader, they didn't dare.

"You've worn it to church. It's already used."

"I haven't worn it to school, have I? I said no, so quit bugging me." Lauren gently blew on her perfect nails. She looked perfect, the way she always did.

My hair was just ordinary looking, and my eyes weren't hazel like Lauren's; they were blue. You know the kind: not green or blue, but somewhere in between. Ordinary. That was why I needed to borrow the sweater so badly. The sweater made my eyes sparkle.

Lauren didn't need anything to make her look special. She could wear an old giveaway from the local used clothing store and still look like a knockout.

Usually, I was proud of Lauren's prettiness. She was one of the most popular girls in the junior class and that was exciting—even if it did make me feel jealous about half of the time.

Most times, she was really nice to me. She was sixteen and had her driver's license. Dad had bought her a car with the understanding that she'd chauffeur me whenever I need a ride, but Lauren had let me trail along with her and her friends other times, too. I never was quite sure whether it was because she liked me, or just felt sorry for me. I didn't dare ask. Sometimes, it was better to leave well enough alone.

Lauren let me borrow her clothes sometimes. That's why I had begged her for the sweater. I was skinnier than her, but her shirts and sweaters fit me okay. That new one was really great looking, so I thought I'd keep trying. Sometimes, if I begged long enough, Lauren gave in, just to shut me up.

"They're going to be taking pictures for the yearbook tomorrow. If you let me wear your new sweater, I'll clean your room after school." I turned my face sideways and gave her a goofy grin—the one that usually made her laugh and give in. It didn't work that time.

"No!" she screamed at the top of her lungs, mean as could be. "Stop acting like such a spoiled brat or I'm telling Mom."

My mouth dropped open. I couldn't believe what she'd said. Red-hot anger flashed through me. I can't ever remember being that mad at my sister.

"I'm not a brat, and telling is something that we agreed never to do. We promised each other." And we never had.

Three years ago when I was eleven and Lauren was thirteen, we'd made a pact that whatever happened between us was secret. "Sacred" was the word that Lauren had used then. We both swore that we'd never rat each other out.

My face grew hot with anger. A flash of fury swept through me, and I was so mad, I thought my teeth would melt. My breath came in short, shallow gasps. I couldn't even speak; that's how furious I was.

I almost blurted out the "b" word, but if Lauren was in the mood to tell on me, that word would get me grounded. Our parents were very strict about what they called "unladylike language." They even sent us to a private Christian school so we wouldn't be exposed to kids using the "F-word." It cost them a bundle of money, but Dad had said that it was worth every penny.

The last thing I wanted was for Lauren's attitude to get me into trouble. I bit down hard on my tongue and watched my snotty sister admire her perfect nails.

"You look like you stuck your fingers into raw liver," I sneered.

Lauren laughed, a hateful tone in her voice.

"What do you know about style?" she snickered. "This is the newest color, and all of my friends are wearing it."

I'd fumed a while longer, scheming about how to get even. Then, something happened that had sent our whole family down a spike-paved road to hell.

My sister rolled over on the bed and her T-shirt flipped up. I saw a tiny roll of fat and I remembered Lauren worrying about her weight earlier in the week.

"At least I'm not fat!" I shouted and watched her eyes widen with pain. There, I thought, satisfied and enjoying that good/bad feeling you get when you hurt someone on purpose. Good because you told them off, bad because your conscience stung. I ignored my conscience. Serves you right, I thought. Now you know how it is to get your feelings hurt. "You look really fat in that new sweater—like a blimp."

I tore out of her room, then stuck my head back in after she thought that I was gone. I could see tears welling in her eyes, but I didn't go back.

The next day, Lauren went on a diet.

Mom seemed real happy about it. She was into health and fitness and was always pushing vegetables and other gross stuff at us.

While Lauren nibbled a salad, I made a big deal of eating a huge mound of mashed potatoes and gravy and a nice slab of roast beef.

"Yummy." I smacked my lips. "Sure am glad that I inherited Dad's skinny genes. Everyone's always telling me that I look just like model material." Actually, that was a big stretch of the truth. Old Mrs. Hilling—who taught English and looked like crap—told me that once, but I figured it was because she felt sorry for me, since I was the plain one in my family.

But Lauren didn't seem to mind. She was back in a good mood and just smiled at me.

"This salad's really good," she said. "It filled me right up."

I figured she was lying. I looked at what she had eaten, and even though the bowl was small, she hadn't even finished it. I shrugged and gave a sly little grin. She'd be sneaking back into the kitchen later on and wolfing down chips and dip.

Six months later, I'd have cleaned her room every day for the rest of my life for that to have been true. That was when I had finally figured out that she was starving herself to death.

And no one knew it but me.

At first, I didn't get too excited over Lauren's strict diet. I figured that she was eating junk away from home. That's what I would have done. I'd have made a big deal of my diet while everyone was watching; then I'd have had a huge fast-food hamburger when no one was looking.

Not my sister!

Lauren had never been into exercise before she started dieting. She'd liked to swim, but that was about all. After she went on her diet, she suddenly turned into a super jock. She was up an hour early every morning working out to an aerobics tape, and every evening, she stopped by Johnson's Swim School, where we had a family membership and practiced laps. I knew, because I had to go along.

I'd put on my suit and splash around a little, sliding down the big slide and playing sharks and minnows with some of the little kids who were around. But Lauren was serious.

The scary part was that I was the only one who noticed that Lauren wasn't eating more than a bite or two at every meal. That was partly because I was with her most of the time, and Mom and Dad were both preoccupied with other things.

Mom had gotten a big promotion at work and usually didn't get home until late. Dad was rebuilding an old car, the same vintage as his birth—1955. He went to the garage the minute he got home, taking only a few minutes to eat.

During that period, Lauren and I were supposed to be cooking supper.

"You girls help me out while I'm learning my new duties," Mom said. "Then I'll soon be making enough money to make sure you both go on to college."

Of course, we'd agreed. We had a great mom, but actually, Lauren did most of the cooking. She liked being in charge of the food. I think that was so she could be real sneaky about not letting anyone know she wasn't eating.

"I'm stuffed from tasting everything," she'd say, and Dad would nod and tell us something about the rebuilt engine he'd just bought. Mom wasn't interested in old cars, so she'd change the subject and talk about how she'd just hired another employee at the cafeteria that she managed.

"I didn't notice you tasting anything," I said, hoping that my folks would pick up on what was happening. Lauren gave me a dirty look and started fussing because I hadn't been any help in the kitchen. Then Mom would get on my case again, so I just put my head down and shut up.

After a while, the owner of the swim school, Mr. Johnson, noticed how hard Lauren was working out. He pulled one of the red ropes down the length of the pool to give her a practice lane. Sometimes, he'd come out and offer her pointers. Then, one afternoon, he asked her to join the Tri-County swim team. He said he would present her name to the coaching committee for consideration. She was thrilled.

Mom and Dad were pleased, too.

"It's such an honor," Mom said, her eyes glowing with pride.

"Takes after her old man," Daddy bragged. "I was always good in sports."

I didn't say anything. I had seen Lauren in her frenzy to exercise every day. I noticed that she played with her food, instead of eating. I'd seen her in her swimsuit and knew how thin she had become.

Looking skinny was fashionable and everyone seemed okay with Lauren's new slimness—everyone but me. I knew that she had never stopped dieting. I knew that she barely ate anything.

I kept thinking that Mom and Dad would notice. I figured that Mom would see that Lauren had a problem and throw a big fit, but she never did. I think she was just too busy.

A couple of times I'd hinted around, but Lauren had threatened to stop driving me to the mall if I kept it up. Anyway, no one paid any attention to what I said, so I decided to shut up.

Then one day at school, Mrs. Hilling assigned a research paper. We had to pick a subject from a list. I read through the list, bored out of my skull. A research paper was the last thing in the world I wanted to do. I saw the word "anorexia" and my heart almost stopped beating.

Even I knew what that meant. We had heard enough about it, and we'd even watched a TV special once when I was in the seventh grade. I remembered anorexia as the disease where people wouldn't eat. Mom had joked about it, saying that she wouldn't mind a mild case of that illness because it was so hard not to gain weight while working at a cafeteria. That was back when my family was normal.

I stared at the word and knew with absolute certainty that anorexia was what Lauren had. I'd selected anorexia for my paper and listened to Mrs. Hilling tell how we could do our research.

That night, I'd pulled up an online search engine on the computer and typed in the word "anorexia." I was given about a gazillion choices, so I'd picked one and begun reading. The more I read, the sicker I felt. The worst thing I learned was that people died from that disease.

My heart pounded. How could that be possible? People didn't starve to death—not in the United States. That was just plain stupid. There was no way that I was going to let that happen to my big sister. Or, so I'd thought.

I grabbed my stash of peanut butter candies—the ones I wouldn't share with anyone, and a new fashion magazine. I marched myself right into Lauren's room. The candy was her favorite, too, and I was going to stop her dieting, right then.

Lauren was sitting at her desk working on her geometry homework with a CD blasting.

"I'm sick of working on that research paper," I lied. "I've found the cutest dress, and I want you to see it. Maybe we can go shopping this weekend and find one just like it. I have some money saved from my allowance." I plopped down in the middle of her bed and spread out the magazine and candy. She looked up with a sigh.

"I'm not buying any new clothes until I lose more weight," she said. "What would be the point?"

"Lose more weight! What are you talking about? You're already skinnier than a rail." I picked up a candy and pulled off the wrapper. "Here," I said. "Have a bite. It's yummy."

Lauren jerked back like I was handing her a maggot sandwich.

"I can't," she said. "I've got to lose some weight. You know I need to stick to my diet."

"Why would you want to lose any more weight? You could hide behind a toothpick!"

"I wish," Lauren said.

I trailed the opened candy under her nose, figuring she'd never be able to resist the yummy chocolate smell. Chocolate had always been her favorite.

"How can you be so mean?" Big tears welled in Lauren's eyes. "Quit making fun of me! You were the one who told me I was fat, and you were right. I'm just trying to do something about it. I hate being so fat." A tear slid down her cheek and dropped on her blue T-shirt.

"What are you talking about?" I jumped off the bed, grabbed my sister, and pulled her to the full-length mirror she had gotten for her thirteenth birthday.

"Look at yourself. You aren't fat. I'll bet if you took off that shirt, I could count your ribs."

"I'm looking and I am fat! Just look at me. Fat is hanging off my body everywhere. Now get out of my room and quit bugging me."

"I'm not bugging you, I'm trying to help. I'm sorry I said you were fat. I was just mad at you because you wouldn't let me borrow your sweater. I didn't really mean it. I was being a jerk and trying to hurt your feelings."

"I know fat when I see it! Get out and take that candy with you or I'm going to spit on every piece."

I grabbed my bag of candy and backed out of her room. Lauren wasn't pretending. She really thought that she was fat. I went back to my room and read some more articles on anorexia that I had downloaded from the websites.

There was an article about a girl who was around Lauren's age and height, which was five-feet-four. She was down to ninety pounds, and said that when she looked into the mirror, she didn't see what other people saw. She saw only fat.

My parents didn't even know that Lauren had a problem.

I crawled onto my bed and curled up into a ball—dirty shoes and all. My sister was dying, and it was my fault. That horrible thought kept racing through my mind.

What was I going to do? If I told our folks, Lauren would quit taking me along when she went really cool places with her friends. Since I wasn't that popular, myself, I'd probably be hanging out by myself most of the time. That thought made me sick to my stomach.

But I had to do something—even if Lauren never spoke to me again. Even if I had to go everywhere by myself: to the mall, the movies, even the school games. I had to try and save my sister.

Mom had a makeshift office set up into the dining room, and that's where I went. She looked tired and busy, with an unhappy frown as she scowled down at a report she was finishing for work.

"What are you doing?" I had been told a million times not to bother her while she was working, but this was an emergency. Mom sighed, rubbed a spot between her eyes, and frowned at me.

"Not now, baby," she said. "I've got to finish this tonight."

I couldn't give up. There wasn't time. "Have you noticed how much weight Lauren has lost?" I asked. There wasn't a minute to lose if I was going to save my sister.

"Yes. Isn't it great? It's always good to lose your baby fat before you're grown." Mom picked up her pencil.

My mouth dropped open and I just stared at Mom. It was a minute before I could even think. I realized that Lauren always wore loose clothes around our folks: oversized T-shirts, billowy tops, or A-line dresses. Mom didn't have a clue that Lauren was killing herself.

"She's losing too much weight," I said.

"You afraid you're not going to be able to borrow her new clothes?" Mom laughed, teasing me.

"No, I'm afraid she's going to starve herself to death and die!"

I watched Mom's face turn pale, and I felt about two inches high.

"That's not funny, Megan. Now quit griping about your sister and go back to your homework."

"I'm not kidding, and I'm not making this up, Mom." I felt my lips begin to quiver, and I couldn't keep tears from streaming down my cheeks. "I think that she's got anorexia. I'm scared that she's slowly starving herself to death."

"Don't be ridiculous!" Mom snapped. "Now go on and finish your homework like I told you."

My feelings were hurt so badly that I ran down the hall and into my bedroom and slammed the door shut. What was wrong with my mother? Was she blind? Didn't she care? I wanted to scream.

Mom surprised me. The next day was Saturday, and after breakfast, she announced she'd taken a spur-of-the-moment vacation day. We were going shopping.

"But, Mom, I always go shopping with my friends," Lauren said.

"Then, isn't it lucky that this time you'll have your mother along to whip out her plastic?" Mom said. Lauren made a couple of other excuses, but Mom wouldn't change her mind. I began to hope.

Mom drove us to the mall and we walked to our favorite department store, where I began grabbing things off the racks, but Lauren held back.

"I'd rather wait until I've lost all the weight I need to lose," she said.

"The new styles are really pretty this year," Mom said. "I want you to each have one new outfit. I insist."

Lauren chose a couple of things, and I noticed they were a size five. I knew that a five would fall off of her, but I didn't say a word.

When we went into the dressing room and Lauren slipped off her shirt and jeans, Mom sucked in a hard breath. I was right. You could see every bone in my sister's body.

After that, things changed fast at my house. I gave Mom all of the stuff I had downloaded from the online search engines. She called our family doctor and made an appointment, making everyone go along—even Dad.

After examining Lauren, Dr. Hill left her in the waiting room and met with the rest of us in his study. I'd gone to him for as long as I could remember, but I'd never seen him this serious.

He said that he'd just learned about a new type of therapy they had been using in England to treat anorexia nervosa, and it involved the whole family.

"The family's job is to try and get Lauren to eat any way you can," Dr. Hill said.

I rolled my eyes. He made it sound so simple, and I knew it was almost impossible. Dr. Hill misunderstood and gave me a real hard look.

"I don't need any attitude from you, young lady," he said. "This is a life-and-death matter. And if you care anything at all about your sister, you'll help with this."

Well, that just went all over me. Here was this old guy giving me a lecture on helping, on caring about my sister. When the only reason we were sitting in his office was because I had ratted her out. I looked over at Mom, expecting her to defend me. But she didn't. She just sat there, staring at the doctor, her eyes huge and filled with terror.

"Die?" Mom said. "Lauren could die?" Mom freaked out,

doubling up as if she had a bellyache. She cried so hard that it took both my dad and the doctor to get her calmed down.

We got our instructions: Lauren had to eat. She could be coaxed, bribed, tricked, or even force-fed. But she had to eat. Mom wasn't even to worry about what she ate. Cookies, junk food, milkshakes— anything was okay to begin with. The trick was to get her to eat.

"According to this new theory, the deprivation of food seems to cause the mind of an anorexia victim to see things differently. When Lauren looks into the mirror, she really sees a fat person." He leaned forward on his polished walnut desk and made a steeple with his fingers. "If she could gain a substantial amount of weight—say, ten or fifteen pounds—her brain would start functioning more normally."

That afternoon, my folks and I had a secret meeting while Lauren was at the movies with her friends. The purpose was to work out what dad called "a game plan." It made me feel important to be included.

"I'll quit working on my car for a while, until Lauren gets better," he said. "You can bet that I'll watch every bite she eats."

"I'm going to get home earlier every evening so I can cook all of her favorite foods," Mom said. "I'll need some help from you in the kitchen, Megan."

"I don't think any of that will help," I said. "I've tried her most favorite food in the whole world, chocolate and peanut butter, and she wouldn't touch it."

"Okay, then. Lauren's always been motivated by money," Dad said. "I'm going to pay her a dollar every time she eats a good meal." He gave me a serious look. "I hope it won't hurt your feelings, because I still expect you to eat for nothing, Megan."

"That's okay." But despite the fact that I wanted Lauren to get well more than anything in the world, something inside me felt kind of empty and jealous. Getting paid to eat? It didn't seem fair.

I remembered how much I loved Lauren and that this whole mess was my fault. If only I hadn't ragged her about being fat. If only I had kept my big mouth shut, then maybe none of this would have happened. Maybe she wouldn't ever have gone on that lousy diet. My stomach twisted into one big knot, and I swore to do everything I could to help Lauren get well—and I wouldn't gripe about it.

Our big "strategy meeting," as Mom called it, turned out to be one huge disaster. Every meal was like living a nightmare.

Mom and I worked our butts off fixing all the things Lauren liked. She just sat at the table, making circles in whatever we fixed with her fork. She smeared food around on her plate, but didn't eat it.

"Please take a bite for me, Lauren," Mom begged, her lips thinning with frustration. "You haven't eaten a thing."

"I can't, Mom; I'm stuffed." Lauren pushed back a plate of

mashed potatoes with gravy, a thick slice of roast chicken, and buttered carrots. It looked so good to me. I could've eaten another plateful, but I'd already had two. Lauren pushed her chair away from the table and stood up.

"You sit right back down, young lady," Daddy yelled, his face growing red and angry. "You're not leaving this table until you've eaten at least seven bites."

"I can't, Daddy. I'm too full. I'd throw it up." Lauren's face settled into the stubborn lines that I'd known my whole life. My sister was sweet and charming, but when she got "that" look on her face, you'd might as well give up and let her do whatever she wanted.

Daddy stood up and stalked around to Lauren. He grabbed her fork, filled it with mashed potatoes, and held it up to her tightly closed lips.

"Open your mouth," my usually sweet and loving father yelled. I wanted to jump up, to hide in my room, to put on the loudest CD I owned. I'd do anything to drown out Daddy's yelling, Mom's crying, and my sister's protests.

"Sally!" Daddy yelled at Mom. "Come and help me with this." Poor Mom walked over to him with a look of horror on her face. He handed her the fork, then proceeded to pry Lauren's jaws open while Mom put the food into her mouth. Both of them had tears running down their cheeks. Daddy held Lauren's mouth shut until she had to swallow.

It's just like when we give Spot his pills, I thought, wanting to puke.

I jumped up, ran back to my room, and slammed the door. My heart pounded as if it were going to burst through my chest—and right then, I wished that it would. I wished that my aching heart would burst and I could just die. Then, the pain and guilt that I was feeling would be over forever.

Hot tears streamed down my cheeks and I sank down onto my bed. Muffled sounds still came from the dining room so I covered my head with a pillow and cried. My family was trapped in hell, and there was no way for us to escape.

It was all my fault.

Time crept by as our once happy home turned into the family from hell. It was easy for Dr. Hill to tell us to force Lauren to eat, but it was something else to make it happen.

We struggled along like that for a couple more weeks, but Lauren wasn't gaining any weight at all. She even seemed to lose a bit more.

The only thing that seemed to calm her were the laps that she still swam every night. I think that Mom and Dad were relieved that there was one thing my sister still enjoyed doing. In fact, she was getting so good, in spite of her weight loss, that Mr. Johnson told her she had been accepted to join the swim team. The coaching committee had approved her. Lauren could join the Tri-County Swim Team when the new session started in about two months. Lauren was thrilled. I hadn't seen her so happy for almost a year.

"I can't believe it," she said as she drove us home. We had stopped at the convenience store as a reward and I was sipping a large frosted drink. Lauren drank bottled water.

"If you'd eat some protein, you'd swim even better." The science nerd in me couldn't keep her mouth shut. I was waiting for that hard look that always came into Lauren's eyes when anyone talked about her eating, but, instead, there was a quick flash of something else—a question, maybe? I began to feel hopeful, but Lauren shook her head.

"I'm already stuffing myself," she said. "What I really need to do is lose a few more pounds. That would put me into shape."

My blood ran cold.

Lauren was so happy and bouncy and so much like her old self when we got home that Mom and Dad perked right up. I could see they also hoped this would be a good thing. We talked about it at supper.

"I'm so proud of you, sweetie," Mom said. "But you've got to get some food inside you. Come on, have one big bite for your old mom."

"Seven bites," Dad said with an already beaten look on his face. He would lose this battle and he knew it.

But an idea had been forming in my mind since that afternoon. Maybe there was a solution. And maybe, just maybe, I had found it.

I sat with my own food untouched—something really unusual for me. My heart pounded and my palms sweated. My idea might just work, but if I spoke up, my sister would feel that I had betrayed her. She'd hate me. I'd never again be included in the fun jaunts with her friends. She might even stop loving me.

Tears filled my eyes and one trickled down my cheek. She might hate me forever, but she would be alive. My heart felt like it was filled with lead and I wanted to throw up, but I opened my mouth and spoke.

"Tell her she can't join!" I said.

Everyone turned and looked at me as if I had grown an extra head.

"What are you talking about?" Mom asked.

"It's not like you to be jealous." Dad's voice sounded disappointed and angry.

"You're such a brat these days," Lauren said.

But I didn't give an inch. My sister's life was at stake.

"Tell her she can't join the swim team unless she gains fifteen pounds." My voice shook and Lauren looked at me as if I had driven a stake through her heart.

Mom and Dad got real quiet. They exchanged a look.

"What a good idea," Dad said. "Thank you, Megan, for the suggestion."

"You can't be serious," Lauren said. "No one would turn down a chance to be on this swim team. Who knows—it might even give me a chance at the Olympics. For sure, it'll get me a scholarship to college."

"Won't do you any good if you're dead," I said.

"I hate you, you rotten little brat!" Lauren screamed. "Just see if I ever do one thing for you again."

That night I cried myself to sleep. My sister was going to despise me forever. Things would never be the same between us. She'd never again be on my side and take up for me when I got into trouble. I had lost the most precious friend I had ever had in my whole life. But she would live. I kept comforting myself with that thought. Whatever else happened, my sister would live.

Lauren did hate me. She barely spoke to me, but she started eating.

My folks let her eat anything she wanted, just as long as it was food. If she wanted to have chocolates and soda for breakfast, that was okay.

Of course, I still had to eat nasty old cereal, like always, but I kept my mouth shut. I sure wasn't going to get any sympathy from Lauren.

She ate potato chips and dip for lunch and brownies and ice cream for supper. But she began to gain weight. A tiny covering of flesh coated her bones and some color returned to her cheeks.

And I had done it.

For the first time since the nightmare had started, I felt good about myself again. My sister was going to live—and because of me!

After Lauren put on about five pounds, Mom quit letting her eat just any kind of junk and demanded that she add some protein, vegetables, and fruit. Sometimes while Lauren ate, she sat at the table and gagged, but we ignored her and pretended that everything was all right. But she kept eating, because more than anything in the world, she wanted to be on that Tri-County swim team.

One night, the craziest thing happened. After Lauren gained ten pounds, her thinking seemed to change. Just like Dr. Hill had said that it might. I slipped into her room one afternoon to see if she might speak to me and she was standing before the mirror in her panties and bra.

"I think that I may actually look okay," she said in an awe-filled voice. I wanted to grab her cheerleading pom-poms and give a yell right then and there.

As Lauren continued to gain weight, she got better both physically and mentally. She was sent to therapy along with our whole family, and when it came time for her to join the swim team, she had gained fifteen pounds and was up to one hundred and five pounds. She wasn't exactly huge, but definitely healthy.

Lauren gradually thawed toward me. I guess she couldn't stay mad at her only sister forever. I was so thrilled the first time she turned to me and said I could come to the movies with her and her friends that I almost cried.

Our family is not out of the woods yet—not by any means. I know that. We all still attend therapy and work hard to keep Lauren healthy. Mealtimes are better.

"When are you going to start paying me to eat?" I said to Dad just last night at upper, giving him a big grin so he'd know I was teasing.

"Are you kidding? The way you're putting away that meat loaf, I'd save money by paying you not to eat."

The intended joke echoed awkwardly in the room, the way words do when you tell a joke and it goes wrong.

Dad's ears turned red, then the color drained out of his face, giving him a weird, splotchy look. He looked so miserable that something in my heart twisted. I knew only too well, how it felt to end up with your foot in your mouth.

"No way is that going to happen," I said, keeping my smile bright to save him from more embarrassment. "Mom's cooking is way too good. You are what you eat, and I intend to be something really special. Like my big sister."

You could have heard a pin drop. Something miraculous happened.

Lauren reached across the table and squeezed my hand.

"I love you, Megan," she said.

Tears stung my eyes and my heart swelled with gratitude. My sister was once again my best friend!

THE END

3 SISTERS, 1 MAN
Who will he choose?

Having two sisters has always been, at the very least, interesting. Sharing an apartment with them? That defies logic. They've never been very good at sharing.

My older sister, Megan, is a junior accountant working on her master's degree at night school. Mandy, the baby of the family, is a sales manager at an upscale women's clothing store. She is pursuing her "Mrs." degree. As for me, I have my path neatly laid out, too. I'm a nurse working the graveyard shift, trying to save enough money to move out on my own.

Since we're never home at the same time, the three of us have been getting along pretty well.

That is, until Tyler Ashford came along.

I knew the man was trouble the first time I saw those eyes and that killer smile. To be fair, it wasn't his fault.

Megan brought Tyler home to review his taxes. The poor guy was being audited. When Mandy got one peek at his estimated earned income, it was all over.

Megan and Mandy were in the kitchen arguing, yet again. All I wanted was a little peace and quiet before I went to work.

"Would you two stop yelling?" I said to them.

"Melissa, please tell Mandy that Tyler is my friend. I will not have him exploited because he earns enough to keep her in the style she would like to become accustomed to," Megan said.

"You're jealous because he's attracted to me instead of you," Mandy shot back, admiring her perfectly manicured nails.

"You had no business looking at his tax forms," Megan said.

"Stop," I demanded.

As though ending round one, the doorbell chimed. Neither of my sisters moved from their corners to answer it. I stomped through the living room and yanked open the door.

He smiled, and in that moment I realized how one man had turned our household into a battleground.

"Tyler." I was talking to myself, but he thought I was greeting him.

"You must be Melissa," he said. "Nice to meet you. Is your sister here?"

"Oh, they're both here," I said. And as if on cue, they appeared.

"Tyler!" my sisters cooed, pushing past me.

"Take your pick," I muttered, grabbing my coat to leave.

When the elevator door opened, I was more than a little surprised to see Tyler right behind me.

"That was quick."

"Just had to drop off some deductions. Besides, it was kind of tense in there."

We stood in awkward silence for a moment as the elevator descended. Then he spoke. "I've always wanted to wear pajamas to work."

I looked down at my pink scrubs and laughed. "I like it."

"Which hospital do you work at?" he asked.

"St. Paul's. I work in the geriatric unit."

"No kidding? My grandmother's there right now, in rehab. She broke her hip. Abby Ashford."

"Miss Abby is your grandmother?"

"None other than."

"I adore her. She's such a great lady."

"I think so, too. In fact, that's where I'm headed."

We were out to the street. "Well, I'll see you there. There's my bus," I said.

"Let me give you a ride," he offered.

I'm not stupid. Of course I took the ride. Saving money on the bus meant it was that much sooner that I could move out of that apartment. And Tyler was great company, too.

"So how come I never see you on my grandmother's floor?" he asked as we drove.

"I normally work nights. Today I'm working a double, covering a swing shift for a friend."

"Nights? You aren't the one who plays cards with Grandma, are you?"

"I've played a few hands of poker with Abby when she's had insomnia. She refuses a sleeping pill, you know."

"I think the word she used to describe you was card-shark."

"Hey, I won those cookies fair and square."

Tyler laughed. "Oh, sure. That's what they all say."

I pretended to be outraged. "I'll prove it to you during my dinner break. Stop at the bakery across from the hospital and I'll run in. We're going to need more cookies."

Bending the rules a tiny bit, I allowed Tyler to stay a little longer than the posted visiting hours. His grandmother enjoyed it. I was sorry to see him leave.

I only wish all my shifts went as fast as that one did. The night shift crept by, and I was only too glad to walk out of the hospital into the fresh air in the morning. In my usual zombie-like morning trance,

I walked along the route home until a car's persistent horn got my attention.

"Hey, Melissa."

It was Tyler.

"Hi there, Tyler. What're you doing here?"

"I wanted to see you again."

"I'm too tired to play cards," I said. "Beside, you won most of the cookies."

"Hop in, I'll take you home."

"No, I'll fall asleep and then you'll have to carry me in the house." I shook my head. "And frankly, I'm no lightweight."

I heard him laugh. A second later he was striding next to me.

"Got any plans for your time off?" he asked.

"You bet. Today, I'm sleeping until noon. And then I'm going to roll over and look at the clock and go back to sleep." I sighed with anticipated pleasure.

"How about a movie tomorrow night?"

"That's a wonderful idea," I said. "You rent the movie, and I'll borrow the VCR from administration. We can make popcorn in the nurse's lounge. Abby will love it."

"That wasn't exactly what I had in mind." He paused. "But sure. Okay."

"What time?" I asked.

"I'll pick you up at six."

"Great!" I dashed into my building, waving good-bye.

That evening I sat on the stairs outside my building, bleary eyed. My sleep was interrupted at eleven by the vacuum cleaner. Megan came home early to clean the house.

She'd invited Tyler over for dinner to celebrate his successful tax audit. I was the first to point out that she didn't make me dinner when she did my taxes. But she didn't hear me over the noise. My sisters were at it again. They were arguing over Tyler.

"Why so glum?"

It was him, standing over me, hands in pockets. He looked wonderful as usual.

"Men," I said.

"Men?"

"Never mind." I stood and linked my arm in his. "I hope you're hungry. Megan has been cooking all day. Be sure to mention the pasta sauce. Oh, and Mandy got her hair done. You'd probably better notice that, too."

"Okay," Tyler said, giving me a quizzical look.

Thanks to Tyler's lavish compliments, dinner went very well. In fact, my sisters called a temporary truce. They decided Tyler liked them each equally, and they were subdued. I knew he was going to have to make up his mind soon.

The next evening I waited for him outside the building. My sisters didn't know Tyler and I had plans. Since their temporary peace was so tenuous, I figured what my sisters didn't know wouldn't hurt me.

We had a lovely time with Abby. When she fell asleep at the end of the movie, Tyler and I quietly slipped out. The night was warm, so we walked.

After ice cream cones, we walked some more. We found an all-night coffee shop and talked for hours. When we realized it was morning, we reluctantly headed back to my apartment.

"Melissa, do you believe in love at first sight?"

"No," I said. "But don't let that stop you. Is it Megan or Mandy?"

"Neither."

I shook my head. "That's not good," I mumbled. My sisters were going to be extremely unhappy.

"What about you and that man you were talking about?" he asked.

"Man? What man?"

"The other night. You were muttering something about men."

"Oh, that was a generic muttering. Why?"

"Melissa." He took my hand. "You are the only sister I'm crazy about."

I didn't know whether to throw my arms around the man or slug him. Did he realize how much trouble I was going to be in?

"Me? Are you sure?"

He laughed. "Of course I'm sure."

"But Megan thinks you're an accountant's dream. You keep alphabetized receipts. And Mandy is in love with your tax bracket."

"And you?"

"Well, of course I like you."

He frowned.

"I more than like you, Tyler. I'm crazy about your grandmother. And I adore playing cards with you. And I could talk to you forever."

"Forever is good," he said, no longer frowning.

We reached my building.

"We should take it slow," I said. "Forever is a long time, you know."

He smiled. "Do you think a kiss would be okay?"

"Have you kissed my sisters?"

"Of course not. I mean, they're nice, but I was waiting to kiss the right sister."

"Good answer," I said, leaning toward him.

It was a good kiss. A forever kind of kiss.

From behind us a terse cough and an astonished gasp ended it all much too quickly.

"Good morning, Megan. Good morning, Mandy. Have a great day," I said, never taking my eyes off Tyler.

And the right sister finished her forever kiss.

THE END

THE LEGEND
OF LOVERS

"Now, you don't mind ghosts, do you, dear?"

Standing on the veranda of the columned, antebellum-style house, I looked from one smiling, seventy-something senior to the other lady, her mirror-image twin. They were serious.

Penelope Blanchard repeated, "I hope you don't mind. They aren't the bad kind of ghosts."

Before I could say anything—and there was a lot I wanted to say—her twin, Polly, piped in. "Just . . . you know, mischievous, sometimes. Well, there is Blake to deal with."

The Blanchard sisters exchanged a look. Polly added, "She needs to know. Just in case."

Penelope hesitated, then smoothed an imaginary wrinkle from her linen dress and straightened to her full height of barely five-foot-three. The faint drawl in her voice became more pronounced as she said, "Our great-great uncle, Blake Blanchard, was a bit wild in his day."

"Blake the Rake, they called him," chirped Polly, beaming up at me.

"He was known to have an eye for the ladies," Penelope said.

"And a hand," Polly murmured, then fell silent at a look from her twin.

It was a joke. It had to be. I looked around, waiting for someone to expose the gag by pointing out people awaiting my reaction. The smiling seniors watched me, then looked around, as if wondering what I was looking for.

"Do you see something, dear?" Penelope asked kindly, but without surprise.

I realized then, that—for these two—this was their reality. A mansion that evidently came complete with hot and cold running ghosts.

I realized something else. By accepting the job, this would now be my reality, too. At least for six hours a day, five days a week.

"Goodness, our manners!" Penelope said crisply. She reached out to touch my arm, gesturing toward the doorway. "Come inside and we'll get acquainted over tea."

Polly smiled and helped her twin usher me into the house. The cool interior reinforced the look of the exterior, with museum-quality furnishings reminiscent of a Savannah plantation home, somehow

148

transplanted here just a half an hour from St. Louis.

As if awaiting her cue, a plump, rosy-faced woman stepped into the foyer, pushing an antique tea trolley. "The ladies' parlor?" she asked.

Penelope nodded, then turned to me. "This is Amelia Hart, our housekeeper."

"A treasure." Polly leaned toward me. "She and Tad, her husband, have been with us forever. We couldn't do without them."

Penelope motioned me forward. "Amelia, this is Gwen Covington. Sebastian has hired her to help us with our projects."

I heard a noise from Polly that sounded suspiciously like a snort, but Penelope ignored it and continued.

"Welcome, Miss Covington," Amelia said, shaking my hand. "If you need anything, just let me know."

"Thank you, and please, call me Gwen," I said, smiling.

After settling us in the room, the housekeeper left. Over tea and the best chocolate chip cookies I'd ever eaten, the ladies asked me about myself. Their charm, interest, and method of questioning lead me to reveal much more than I had intended to. Within a surprisingly short time, Penelope and Polly Blanchard knew that I was twenty-five, divorced, with a six-year-old daughter, Melissa, who had a deadbeat dad who'd disappeared from our lives three years before. I found myself telling them about my parents' deaths the year before my marriage, my brother, who lived in California, our move here, and my struggle to balance making a living being a mom and keeping up with the business classes I was taking in my spare time at the local community college.

Suddenly, I realized how much I was revealing. Reaching for another cookie, I decided it was time to ask my own questions. "Miss Blanchard," I started, then paused when both silver heads tipped in response.

Penelope smiled. "That won't do, you know. Since there are two Miss Blanchards, you must call us by our names, and we shall call you Gwen."

"All right, then," I said, taking a sip of the tea. "Penelope, as you know, your law firm hired me from the Harbor Home Health Service to assist you. They were clear on salary, hours, and benefits, but not the exact duties. Can you give me an idea of what I will be doing?" I'd already pegged Penelope as the more serious, responsible one of the pair of aged "belles."

"Well, dear, just as we told Amelia, you will be helping us with our projects."

Before I could ask just what that involved, Polly piped in, as she seemed to enjoy doing. "And spy on us for Sebastian."

"Polly, hush," Penelope chided. "You know better than that."

"Sister, you said so yourself, too," Polly retorted. "But I don't think it's true." She looked at me, and solemnly pronounced, "I like you, Gwen. You are no spy."

Feeling like a Ping-Pong ball, I let my gaze—and open mouth—swing back to Penelope as she said, "Yes, I agree, Polly. You are no spy, dear. And I, too, like you."

"In fact," Polly said, tilting her head to stare at me, "I think she's ideal. Don't you, Sister?"

After exchanging a long look with her twin, Penelope nodded, a slight smile curving her lips. "Why, yes, I believe you're right," she drawled.

I snapped my mouth shut, determined to crawl out of the hole I seemed to have fallen into and take control of the situation. Little did I realize then, that control was something I forfeited the moment I walked into the Blanchard household. But I wasn't about to leave. The job was simply too good a deal to pass up in my situation.

When I moved here, I'd signed on as a companion/homemaker with the home health service because the hours were flexible enough to work around my daughter's school and my own classes. The pay wasn't great, but we got by. Then I was called in by the supervisor and told I'd been recommended to the law firm of Blanchard, Charles, and Kluer, who were handling the affairs of two elderly ladies and seeking a personable, trustworthy young woman to act as companion and driver.

The job was to be Monday through Friday, from eight o'clock in the morning until three in the afternoon. With the hour off for lunch, it came out to only six hours a day, thirty hours a week. And, not only would I get forty-hour-a-week pay—which was noticeably more than I was making full-time—but I'd also get paid family insurance, including vision and dental. It took only a minute to snap it up. Not only would I make more money for less work, I'd save wear and tear on my car by not having to drive to one place after another each day, and I'd save on the cost of our insurance that had been deducted from each check.

I tried to shake off my thoughts of It sounds too good to be true. "I don't know anything about being a spy. And who is Sebastian?" I asked the ladies.

Penelope settled back in her wing chair. "Sebastian is our baby brother, Ethan's, grandson—our great nephew."

I had to hide a smile at Penelope—who had to be seventy-five if she was a day—calling Ethan her "baby brother."

"Ethan is a widower, and he lives in Florida. He plays golf and generally makes a fool of himself with the ladies there," Penelope continued calmly. "His son, Charles, is on his fourth marriage—"

"Fifth," Polly corrected, reaching for another cookie.

"Oh, yes, I forgot the travel agent. Anyway, Charles is in California doing things with computers and collecting more wives. Sebastian is his only son. He lives here, in St. Louis, and is a lawyer, like his grandfather."

"He worries about us," Polly added. "That's where you come in."

"But what does he want me to do?" I all but wailed, trying to wade through the genealogy to get to the heart of the matter: Sebastian, my boss, and my duties as his employee.

I think Penelope realized how overwhelmed I was feeling. She spent the next few minutes describing the charities they worked with, some of the things they did on a weekly or monthly basis, and a few of the projects they had in mind.

"We're busy now with fundraisers to purchase thermal imaging equipment for the fire department," Penelope said. "We also have some old family papers to organize, and we're planning to redecorate the rose bedroom."

"Olivia won't like that," Polly muttered.

After a stern look at her twin, Penelope continued, "We also need to make a video inventory of each room, as we are working with our insurance people before making some bequests in our wills. You'll help us with these things."

"A piece of cake," Polly said, and winked.

It turned out she was absolutely right. In the next couple of weeks, I found myself relaxing in a way I hadn't in years. The workload the "girls"—as they enjoyed being called—had for me was so light that I felt a little guilty each time I cashed a paycheck. My daughter, Melissa, delighted in her new, more relaxed mommy as well. Being a single mom was a real stress, and now that I had more time—and more money—our life was definitely improved.

Although I hadn't yet met their nephew, Sebastian, I spoke to him once every week. He would call me at home, and I found him to be as aloof as his aunts were friendly, but there was no denying his concern about his elderly relatives. He always wanted to know about what we had done, and if the sisters had mentioned any problems or health concerns to me.

"I know they don't want to 'bother me' with any ailments," he said. "So I am depending on you to let me know if there is anything to be concerned about."

"They are shockingly healthy," I replied. "And amazingly active and fit for their ages. Sometimes they wear me out!"

It was true. I was always tired, it seemed. Although I took Melissa out for exercise and to the park, I didn't do much exercise, myself. But going with Penelope and Polly on their daily walks had made a difference that I could feel in my energy level.

After he hung up, I found myself thinking about him. Was he just the worrying kind, or was there some reason for his weekly questions about their health? For some reason, his repeated health questions bothered me. Both sisters had some sinus problems and occasionally took over-the-counter medication for that, but neither needed any prescription medicines, and that was pretty impressive considering their ages. Since they said their brother was also in excellent health, I'd put it down to good luck in the genetic draw.

As time went on, I settled into a comfortable routine with the Blanchard sisters. At their request, I ended up having breakfast with them each morning when I arrived at eight after dropping Melissa off at school. Before, I'd settle for gulping down a cup of coffee while getting Melissa fed and ready for school.

For all their initial warnings, I found I didn't bump into ghosts and ghouls around every corner of the home as I'd feared. In fact, I didn't see anything at all. And if sometimes I felt a strange chill in a room, or a door shut when there was no breeze or a knickknack abruptly tumbled off a shelf, well, I knew there had to be a perfectly logical explanation, and I chose to simply ignore the incidents.

Life was pretty good, I decided one morning, as I brought the car around to take the ladies into a charity meeting. I was getting an education part-time through a displaced homemakers grant program, and got more sleep because Penelope and Polly urged me to bring my textbooks and study while I waited for them at meetings. The extra money meant we didn't have to rely on our old standby of four-for-a-dollar box dinners and five-for-a-dollar canned vegetables. Amelia, the Blanchards' housekeeper, loved to cook, and at least once a week sent home leftovers with me, at the ladies' request. The outdoor exercise had done more than build some muscle; there was an attractive hint of color on my usually pale skin. All in all, even I could see the improvement in my appearance with more sleep, a healthier diet, and less stress.

The only thing missing in my life was love.

After my divorce, I was hurt too much to even think about a romance. Then, making a life for my daughter consumed all my time and energy. Now, the nights began to seem more empty and lonely. I decided to let myself be open to the possibility of a relationship, and when a guy from one of my classes asked me out, I accepted. Nothing clicked between us, but at least I was back out there and began to sporadically date again.

One morning, I pulled my old car back behind the Blanchard manor and went in the back door to greet Amelia in the kitchen before heading to the breakfast room for breakfast with the ladies. But I stopped short when I came through the doorway.

Balloons and crepe paper streamers decorated the small, sunny room, and the table was decorated festively as well. Even the girls were decorated! Penelope managed to make her paper party hat look chic. She had such innate style, but Polly had added a few too many decorations to her party hat, including some glitter, which sparkled in her curly gray hair.

"Happy birthday, Gwen!" they chorused.

"But—but, how did you know?" I managed. I'd even forgotten! There hadn't been much time, or cause, to celebrate in the past.

"We snooped," Polly admitted cheerily. "We asked your former employer to check his records."

"You've been so good for us." Penelope smiled. "We wanted to surprise you."

"I've been good for you? You have it backwards. This is so sweet!"

"You have a very special place in our hearts," Penelope said, motioning for me to sit down in front of several small wrapped boxes. "Had we ever given in to one of our proposals, you might be our granddaughter."

"Why haven't either of you married?" I asked, without thinking. "Oh, I'm sorry; that's really none of my business."

Polly laughed merrily. "It's a question people in this town have asked themselves for . . . oh, decades, dear!"

Penelope smiled and spoke with a hint of feminine pride, "We've certainly had our share of beaus over the years. Polly and I still entertain the occasional gentleman caller. But when it came to marriage. . . ." She looked at her sister.

"We didn't want to be apart, you see," Polly said softly. "And as I'm sure you've come to see, we're far too independent to be good Southern wives."

"And we would feel that lack of wifely duty, even if the family hasn't actually lived in the South since coming here after the War."

I understood the war she referred to had nothing to do with the wars I had grown up hearing about. They explained that after their plantation was destroyed during the Civil War, the Blanchards had moved West to St. Louis, along with assorted spectral ancestors, and begun to rebuild their fortunes.

"We don't like to be told what to do," Penelope said crisply. "And husbands have a way to wanting to do that."

"We have each other." Polly smiled at her sister. "And that's quite enough for us. And after all, we do still get to enjoy romance now and then," she said, winking at me. "The local gentlemen still like to squire around the Blanchard debutantes!"

"Now," Penelope said, closing the subject, "open your gifts."

"This one is for Melissa, so she gets a present, too," Polly said, handing me a pretty gift bag. Inside was a stuffed bunny fashioned of soft, bumpy chenille fabric.

"Oh, she'll love it! Thank you." Polly, I'd discovered, was practically a couture-level seamstress. She designed and made many of the fashions she and her sister wore. She had occasionally given me something she "whipped up" for Melissa, as well.

Penelope's hobby, and special gift, was gardening. Her work in the large greenhouse out back produced the most beautiful flowers, and delicious vegetables, for the table.

After unwrapping a pair of pearl earrings and bottle of perfume, I opened an envelope to find inside an index card with the words "spa day" on it.

"Girls' day out!" Polly laughed. "We're all spending the day at La Bocu!"

La Bocu was the city's most exclusive salon. It would take a week's salary to even think of walking in their door! "That's too much," I protested. "These gifts are enough—more than enough."

Penelope waved away my words. "It's decided, dear. We want to have a special day and we want to share it with you."

I'd experienced the Blanchard will before, and knew the matter was settled.

The day was one I would never forget. We were ushered in as if visiting royalty, although I supposed the Blanchard ladies usually received that kind of deference. From facials to pedicures, we did it all. I even agreed to a complete makeover.

I think even the girls were surprised by the difference a really good hair cut made on me. I know I was. And the make-up artist had brought out my eyes, then showed me how to achieve the same affects and presented me with a selection of cosmetics like the ones she used—a gesture I was sure the sisters had ordered.

"Lovely," Polly breathed. "Just lovely."

Penelope nodded, and said, "You've blossomed, dear."

Looking in the mirror, I could see how right she was. It wasn't just the new hair or make-up, or even that I was eating better, exercising more, and worrying less. It was the ladies. The sense of family I felt being with them. A feeling of security, safety, and love.

As if reading my mind, Penelope leaned over and pressed a cheek against mine. "Yes, dear, for us, too."

As we walked outside, I noticed a man abruptly exiting a doorway across the street and hurrying to his parked vehicle. I barely got an impression of him, but his vehicle did catch my eye, because it was familiar. In an area where vans, town cars and SUVs reigned supreme, the little lime green sports car with the American flag taped to the antenna stuck out like a sore thumb. And at that moment, I realized why.

I'd seen it before—pulling away from the Blanchard place occasionally as I approached to come to work. And I realized I sometimes saw it near wherever I was with the ladies. When I thought of it, I was almost certain that little car had been there the week before, when I'd dropped the ladies off at a charity luncheon. And the week before that when we delivered the boxes of canned goods to the food pantry near the lawyer's office when they'd been in making changes to their wills—too often to be a coincidence.

"What kind of car does your nephew, Sebastian, drive?" I asked, as we got into the car.

Penelope said, "He has several vehicles, I believe. One of those drive-in-the-mountains things, and of course, the luxury car we bought him."

"And that one he calls the 'bug,'" Polly piped in. "That little green car."

It appeared Sebastian was, on occasion, following us—but why? Then I remembered his question-laden weekly phone calls. He was either suspicious of me, and I couldn't imagine why he would be, or, since I spent so much time with his great aunts, he wanted to be absolutely certain I was dependable and trustworthy in my driving. That was probably the reason; he was just being very cautious. Well, he had a right to be that way if he wanted, so I tried to shrug off the feeling of unease that lingered.

Heading back to their home, we talked about the treatments we'd enjoyed at the spa and how we all loved my new hairstyle.

"I'm sure your beau will comment on your new look," Polly said.

There seemed to be the briefest moment of held-breath silence between the ladies, and I know I didn't imagine the look of inquiry in Penelope's eyes. Curious as cats, they were.

"I don't have a steady beau at the moment," I told Polly. Instead of looking crestfallen as I'd imagined, she seemed quite unperturbed, as did Penelope.

But all Polly said was, "You're so fetching, they'll be lining up."

Once back at the Blanchard manor, I followed the ladies in, carrying in their purchases and my own small gift bag of cosmetics from the spa. As I set the packages down on a table in the foyer and turned to close the door, I felt the slightest brush of pressure over my bottom. I swung around with a start. Penelope and Polly were yards away, about to enter the ladies' parlor. They looked at me.

"What is it, dear?" Penelope asked, turning toward me.

"Nothing, I just—" I broke off as the sensation happened again, this time the distinct feeling of a hand brushing the curve of my breast. Gasping, my hand going to my chest, I jumped back. "What the—"

"Oh, dear, we're not the only ones to notice how lovely you look," Polly said, clasping her hands.

Penelope gave a distinctly unladylike sniff and stalked down the hall toward me.

"Blake," she called out, looking up and around. "Stop it this instant! We will not stand for this kind of behavior. Gwen is a guest in our home, and you are not to bother her."

Polly pattered over, leaned in, and whispered, "It's a compliment, dear, really. He doesn't . . . um, express himself with every woman, you know."

"Blake the Rake?" I asked weakly, remembering their description of their womanizing ancestor.

"Harmless, really." Polly sighed. "But I imagine he can be just a bit unnerving."

"Annoying is more like it," Penelope said. "But if you're firm with him, he'll not bother you," she said to me. "Just tell him to leave you alone if it happens again."

I wanted to protest that it had merely been a gust of wind or a trick of my imagination, but I couldn't. What I'd felt hadn't been wind, or my imagination. What it had been, I didn't want to acknowledge.

"Now if it were Olivia," Polly said, "that would be a—"

Penelope interrupted, "I think that can wait for another time."

I was certain it could. I didn't want to hear about any more ghosts!

A week or so later, my summer day-care provider called to tell me she couldn't take Melissa for the day because she had the flu and was going to the doctor. I called the Blanchard house to let them know why I couldn't work.

"Just bring Melissa here with you," Penelope offered. "We'd love to meet her."

"Oh, I couldn't," I protested. "She's quite a handful at times."

"Nonsense. It will be fun."

And, surprisingly, it was. Melissa just soaked up all the attention and affection lavished on her by Penelope and Polly. The housekeeper, Amelia, invited Melissa into the kitchen to help her make cookies while I took the ladies to an appointment. When we returned, we decided to enjoy the results of Amelia and Melissa's labor with a tea party out in the gazebo.

We lazed the summer afternoon away in the shadowed, vine-covered gazebo on padded, wrought iron loungers, drinking lemonade and munching on cookies. With Penelope's blessing, and help,

Melissa raided her flowerbeds and fashioned crowns of flowers for each of us to wear, before running off to chase butterflies.

"She's a delight," Penelope said, smiling at me.

"The love of my life," I agreed. Melissa was the only good thing to come of my disastrous marriage.

"It makes me yearn for grandchildren," Polly sighed. "Not that I particularly wanted children, but oh, how I miss having grandchildren."

We all laughed at her declaration. I got up. "I'd better check on her. With that girl, too much silence can mean mischief."

"Take a hat, dear," said Penelope, as she handed over the floppy, wide-brimmed hat she'd worn while helping Melissa pick flowers. "Mind your complexion."

I accepted the hat, but decided not to put on the sandals I'd kicked off. It was a barefoot kind of summer afternoon to me, so I started off across the grass and along the fieldstone paths of the large, meandering gardens, looking for a glimpse of my daughter. We were wearing similar long, loose, peasant-style flowered gauze dresses that Polly had made for us, but mine was mint color with peach flowers while Melissa's was bright white with little violets. After I got out of sight of the gazebo, I swept off the hat. It was a pretty thing, white straw decorated with pastel flowers around the brim and multicolor trailing ribbons, but I didn't want to crush the circlet of flowers Melissa had made for me, so I just carried the hat as I walked along.

"I see you, Mommy, but you can't see me."

"Melissa? Where are you?"

"Find me, Mommy. Catch me!"

Her giggles danced in the air as she took off, and I caught a glimpse of white beyond a tumble of tall flowering shrubs.

Hide-and-seek at the playground was a favorite, free entertainment we shared, but Penelope's extensive gardens held many more shadowed spots and hiding places than I was used to.

Laughing and hurrying after her, I called out, "I'm going to get you!" and raced around a weeping willow.

I didn't see the other person until a moment before we collided. I went sprawling.

"I'm sorry. I heard you but didn't see you—let me help you up," the man said, reaching down and pulling me to my feet.

Still gripping Penelope's floppy hat, I stared up at him, trying to catch my breath.

He's not a handsome man, I found myself thinking, so how can he seem so good looking? His average looks were illuminated by lively interest in his deep eyes, by a ready smile that crinkled his mouth and eyes, and by an aura of honesty and stability and goodness.

I shook off the strange thoughts and laughed. "It's my fault; I was chasing my daughter and not really paying attention to where I was running."

"You must be Gwen," he said. "I'm Sebastian Blanchard."

Oh, no! For a moment I felt paralyzed. Here was the man who, in effect, was my boss, and while on duty, I was running around with my child in his garden barefoot with . . . I gulped, reached up, and dragged off my crown of flowers. How could he be the stuffy, middle-aged lawyer I'd envisioned, chasing his youth with the lime green sports car? This man couldn't even be thirty!

"But . . . but you're not old," I blurted, then gasped, a hand going to my mouth. "I—I mean . . . oh, I'm sorry."

"You're sorry I'm not old?"

Was there a twinkle in his eyes or not? I could swear there was.

"No, I meant I never expected you to be my age—oh, you know what I mean."

Sebastian laughed, letting me off the hook. "I'm the product of my father's fourth, late-in-life marriage." He grinned down at me. "He was the oldest dad at Little League. I was so embarrassed."

For a long moment, he watched me. I said nothing, nervously clutching the brim of Penelope's hat and my crown of flowers. Trying to say something in the silence, I blurted out, "Have you been following us?"

His eyes narrowed and I wished I could have thought of something—anything—else to say to him, but the question couldn't be taken back now. Instead of the reprimand I expected, Sebastian smiled. "You're quick. I thought you caught on to me after your day at the spa."

"I'm a good driver," I defended myself.

"I know you are. I wasn't concerned about that." He hesitated, seeming to come to a decision, then motioned to a nearby stone bench.

We sat down and he turned to me. "My great aunts are very sharp. Penelope, especially. One of their 'projects' is the stock market, and she and her group of lady friends have made a very, very tidy profit at it. You've heard of the term 'steel magnolias?'"

I nodded. I'd seen this aspect of the women firsthand.

"Well, the girls are steel magnolias, indeed. Very tough. Very smart. And," he paused, looked hard at me, "very lonely. I don't get to visit as often as I'd like. They have plenty of acquaintances, a couple of close friends, and of course, their beaus, but they don't have a lot of what they love: family."

"I don't understand. What does that have to do with me? What does that have to do with following me?"

He shrugged. "It's the same reason why I call to discuss them with you each week. Their loneliness makes them vulnerable to someone who might use that to a disadvantage." He sighed. "I wanted someone to help them a bit, be with them, but I had reservations. Steel magnolias or not, they might be swayed into, say, disastrous business choices by someone charming, charismatic, convincing—"

"And conniving," I finished for him.

"Exactly. They've been dabbling with their wills and various bequests, and I wanted to make certain the details were handled truly as they wanted, not as they might be talked into by—"

"By me?"

"I began to see that your supervisor's assessment of your sterling character was absolutely accurate," he said hurriedly. "And, before you can think badly of me, I want to assure you that I make a very good living at what I do and have a trust fund from my late mother as well, so I could care less what the girls do with their estate."

He seemed concerned that I might be angry at his investigation of me, but I could see that his concern was logical. I was a stranger spending a considerable time with his relatives. I could see, too, that he wanted to let me know his concern wasn't for his own personal gain.

"Mommy! You didn't find me!"

Melissa raced up, then stopped short when she saw Sebastian. Introductions were made and I watched my daughter turn on the charm as if she were a Southern belle in training, offering to show Sebastian the goldfish pond and the hummingbird feeder. He went along, good-naturedly, and the three of us ended up back at the gazebo a few minutes later.

Polly and Penelope exclaimed over Sebastian's appearance and fussed over him with lemonade and cookies. Melissa offered to make him a flower crown, too, and he managed to say no in a way that charmed her completely. In truth, me as well.

That sunny summer afternoon in the gazebo signaled a change at the Blanchard manor. Despite his heavy caseload, in the next couple of weeks, Sebastian managed to make an appearance several times while I was there. Each time, the aunts maneuvered it, quite blatantly, so that Sebastian and I would have time alone. He didn't seem to mind, so I luxuriated in the chance to know him better. And his weekly phone calls took on a completely different content. After checking on his aunt's health and needs, the talk turned to books, movies, likes and dislikes, plans, and dreams. He even asked Melissa to get on the phone each time so they could talk.

I couldn't figure him out, though. He seemed interested in me, yet he never asked me out on a date. He seemed to want to see me only during the day. He never even tried to kiss me when we were alone. In my dark moments, I brooded that he was amusing himself in the daytime with the hired help while he dated rich beauties around town at night.

One Monday, Sebastian came with papers for his aunts to sign. While they were going over them, Penelope suggested Sebastian and I take a walk in the garden and view her new perennial beds. We chatted about nothing and everything as we walked, and as we stepped onto the tiny wooden bridge that spanned the goldfish pond, he moved closer to me and reached for my hand.

We paused at mid-point on the bridge and looked down at the colorful orange and white goldfish below. Even though I kept telling myself he was merely toying with me before he got engaged to someone of his own financial and social circle, I decided to let myself savor every bit of the moment—the closeness of his body, the way his eyes crinkled when he smiled down at me, and the citrus tang of his aftershave overlaid by the heady scent of roses from the gardens.

"You're happy here, with us, aren't you?" he asked quietly.

"Of course." How could he think otherwise? Not only was I— against my better judgment—falling head over heels in love with him, I had grown to love Penelope and Polly as if they were family. I didn't even mind the occasional rocking chair moving when no one was in it, or a book coming open and pages turning when the windows were closed. Even Blake the Rake had been behaving himself.

"Good," he said quietly, smiling.

I breathed in the fragrance of the roses, and knew I would always equate the scent of roses with this captured moment in time on the little bridge with Sebastian.

After he left, Polly slyly asked me if I liked her sister's new perennial bed. Trying to conceal a blush, I didn't want to admit we went no further than the goldfish pool, so I quickly said, "Oh, yes, just beautiful, Penelope. Especially the roses. So fragrant. What kind are they?"

I'd hoped to divert their attention, but it worked in a way I'd never have imagined. Penelope gave a little gasp and turned pale. Polly paled as well, then color swept into her face as she beamed at me. Then she turned to her sister, nodded in satisfaction.

"Olivia."

Penelope sighed. "Sister, you know that is nonsense."

Polly tilted her chin. "Then explain it."

I looked from one to the other. "Explain what?"

Polly looked at her twin. "Olivia's roses. You smelled roses."

I knew I probably looked as confused as I felt. "Yes, but so what? Your gardens are full of flowers."

Penelope looked at me. "Yes, but not roses, dear."

160

I stared back at her. "Well, I'm no gardener like you, Penelope, but I do recognize the fragrance of roses. I know what I smelled out there was roses."

"That's wonderful," Polly beamed, clapping her hands. "New love blooming!"

Penelope shook her head, then sighed. "You might as well tell her," she said to her twin sister. "You're just bursting to do so."

Polly hurried over and settled beside me on the sofa. "The legend of Olivia," she announced breathlessly, "is about love. Love and roses."

She patted my hand. "Olivia was our great-great grandmother, born to Hardy and Mona Blanchard so late in their marriage they despaired of ever having children. They absolutely adored her, and the child was 'pure love,' they say. She was so very loved that she radiated love to all those around her. In time, Olivia chose a distant Blanchard cousin over her many beaus and he built her the Blanchard mansion in Savannah that was destroyed in the War. They say he courted her till the day she died, and then couldn't bear to be without her. He died the day after her funeral."

"It's a lovely story," I said, "but what does it have to do with roses?"

Polly smiled. "I'm getting to that, child. Now, Olivia was blessed with a green thumb. Penelope inherited gardening talent from her, I'm certain. But Olivia's great gift was in growing roses. They say it was as if the love that shined from her glowed in every rosebush she planted; her roses were the talk of three counties. Olivia said roses were an earthly symbol of love. How love, when nurtured, buds and blossoms and fills the world with beauty."

Penelope interrupted. "However, unlike Olivia, I have no talent for roses at all. That's why there are no rose beds here."

"But I know I smelled roses," I protested.

"Yes," Polly said smugly, "you did. That's where the legend comes in. Not only was Olivia legendary for the great love she inspired and for her roses, but they say that ever since then, when a 'forever kind of love' is being born, the couple will be surrounded by the fragrance of roses."

It was a pretty story, and for a moment, it made me feel as if fairytales just might come true, then reality sank back in. Sebastian hadn't said a thing about smelling roses. I'd smelled them, but he evidently hadn't, so what did that mean?

As far as that went, now I questioned whether I'd really smelled the roses at all. I'd been so certain before, but now. . . .

The sisters didn't say anything more—about Olivia, the legend, or the roses—but the rest of the day I caught them eyeing me, then looking away when I caught them at it. The more I thought about it, the more I questioned my own memories of the incident. But I kept thinking about the legend, about a "forever love" being born—signaled by the scent of roses. Finally, I couldn't stand it. I called Sebastian at the office, something I'd never done before. After his secretary transferred me and he picked up the phone, I blurted out, "I have to see you tomorrow."

"Of course, Gwen, is something wrong?"

Oh, I hadn't thought about that—a reason for seeing him, other than testing out the rose legend. But I couldn't tell him the truth. There had to be some convincing.

"The sisters. I have to talk to you about Penelope and Polly."

"Are they okay?" Concern sharpened his voice.

"Oh, yes, yes, they're fine—it's just that . . ." I was scrambling for time. "I can't talk about it here, over the phone, you see."

"Fine, then I'll stop by tomorrow morning."

"No, that won't do," I said hurriedly. I needed to get him alone somewhere without flower gardens nearby. "We're shopping in the morning." We weren't, but I'd convince them we needed to go to the grocery store somehow. "Can you meet us in the parking lot at the SuperSaver about ten?"

He agreed and hung up. I finished up the day and left for home a nervous wreck. The next morning after dropping Melissa at day-care, I hurried to work, and after breakfast tackled the task of getting the girls to agree to a shopping trip without telling them why. I didn't want more speculation from them about roses and love and Sebastian; I was doing enough of that myself.

"You know, I heard the Food Pantry was running low on donations," I mentioned with what I hoped was a casual tone. "Evidently donations are higher near the holidays—Thanksgiving to Christmas—and the rest of the year it slows down."

"We should do another collection this month," Penelope said. Polly nodded.

I felt guilty for a moment, although I had heard a recent public interest story about how food donations usually fell off during summer months. So, I reasoned, their extra donation this month would be put to good use. I also reasoned that there was no way I could smell roses in the middle of a concrete parking lot.

After driving to the SuperSaver and letting the ladies out at the door, I parked the car. I'd told them I had a report due for my summer class and needed a few minutes to make some corrections I'd thought of, then I would join them inside. It wouldn't take long to test my rose theory—the theory being that it was all in my imagination, that I had smelled Penelope's flowerbeds and simply mistakenly thought of the fragrance as roses.

162

A few minutes later, Sebastian drove up in his favorite lime green car. He got out and walked over to where I stood, leaning against the car.

"Hi, Gwen." He smiled.

Oh, that smile of his. Did he realize how it made my heart pound? Of course, he didn't.

"So what's up with the girls?"

For a moment I stared at him blankly, then I remembered that was supposedly the whole point of his meeting me here. Quickly I said, "They want to build a museum. Yes, a museum, and I wondered if you were aware of these plans." Please, I thought, don't let him say anything to them about this. He leaned back against the car beside me, jamming his hands in his pockets, head down.

"They probably aren't serious," I quickly added, so he wouldn't investigate it further. "I shouldn't have bothered you with this." I tried to subtly edge closer and sniff the air as I spoke. "You know how they can get with their 'projects' and enthusiasms. I'm sure it was just a—" I gasped.

The scent of roses! There was no mistaking it! Here, in the middle of the parking lot, the lush fragrance of roses was in full bloom. Sebastian still stared down at the ground, as if lost in thought. "Don't you smell—" I broke off.

He looked up, his face without expression. "Smell what?"

I felt my shoulder slump. So what does that mean, Olivia, I thought, when only one person smells the roses?

Wanting to cry, I made excuses and sent Sebastian on his way, and then went in to join the sisters in their food-buying binge. The day seemed to take forever to get over with.

Just as I was leaving that afternoon, I heard a screech of tires as Sebastian raced into the driveway. He jumped out of the car and came toward me. He'd changed from his suit into jeans and a shirt, so he obviously wasn't working now. He grabbed my hand.

"Gwen—I have to talk to you," he said, pulling me along and into the gardens. He stopped at the crest of the small wooden bridge over the goldfish pool. Then he turned to me. "What did you smell today at the SuperSaver?"

"What?"

"You said you smelled something at the parking lot. What was it?"

I looked down, shaking my head, feeling tears threaten yet again.

"Was it roses?"

I gasped, and my eyes flew to his. There was a wicked glint in his gaze. "Yes," I said slowly. "I smelled roses."

"The Legend of Olivia." He nodded, and smiled.

163

"Yes! Polly told me about it."

"I knew she would," he said. "She loves that story. That's why I thought it would work. But then you wouldn't admit you smelled the roses."

I found it hard to catch my breath. Was he saying . . . "Then—you mean, you smelled them, too?"

He grinned at me, but shook his head. "Of course. Because I did it. It was me, not Olivia. Not some silly legend."

"I don't understand."

He took my hands. "I know you've had some hard knocks and you're wary of relationships, so when I realized I was falling for you, I wanted to go slow." A lopsided grin came and went. "I guess I kinda wanted to court you, like they used to do in Polly and Penelope's day."

A shiver raced along my spine and I felt my heartbeat quicken.

He continued, "But I kept getting mixed signals from you. One minute I was sure you were flirting with me, the next you would seem to pull back."

"I thought you were just having fun with the 'help' before marrying some society beauty," I said breathlessly.

He gave me a mock glare. "That's not my style, Gwen."

Then he grinned. "I knew the twins approved of us being together. After all, I could see they were making you one of their 'projects' practically from the moment you arrived."

I thought back to their efforts to improve my diet, get me exercising, Polly's casual fashion advice, the spa day makeover, and realized how they'd done exactly as he said.

"Anyway," he added, "I decided I needed to help our relationship along and I remembered the Olivia story."

"But Penelope doesn't grow roses," I protested. "She says she can't grow them so there aren't any roses here and I know I did smell them."

"Of course you did. Because I came prepared to make you believe the legend. Both times I had a pocket full of rose petals. All it took was a quick squeeze and the fragrance was released."

"Sebastian!"

"I had to do it." He gathered me into his arms and lowered his head, saying huskily, "I love you, Gwen."

"Oh, Sebastian, I love you, too." I sighed, as his lips claimed mine.

As we shared the first of a lifetime of kisses, the heady scent of roses blossomed around us. I leaned back in his embrace, smiling. "Sebastian, you don't need roses anymore to convince me."

He sniffed the air and a strange look came over his face. Then he said quietly, "I didn't bring any rose petals this time."

164

We looked at each other, wide-eyed, and the smell of roses grew stronger.

Sebastian looked up, said quietly, "Thank you, Olivia," then bent to kiss me again.

The timeless scent of roses—the fragrance of "forever" love—settled over us like a seal of approval. Like a blessing.

THE END

MY SISTER STOLE
MY BOYFRIEND

It was the night before the big bake sale. My sister, Ramona, and I were excitedly making our cookies and brownies. The bake sale was an annual event in our town, held for the benefit of a local children's agency. In order to make it appealing for those us single women, the bake sale featured an old-fashioned basket lunch auction. Single women generally prepared tasty baskets for adoring men—the woman hoped there would be an adoring man.

Each woman was given a number. The number corresponded with the basket. And, of course, the woman would make her number known to those men that she wanted to bid on her. It was supposed to be a secret, but it wasn't really. The more popular women would have several men bid on her basket. Sometimes the bedding became furious.

Not being one of the popular girls, I always considered myself lucky just to get one guy to bid on my lunch. And this year was no different from the others. Marshall Lassiter was my date. I wasn't too crazy about him, but having a date was better than not having one at all. A girl who couldn't get a box lunch partner just didn't rate.

That's why, when Ramona inquired casually, "Who's going to bid on you, Jeanette?" I had a hard time keeping the bitterness out of my voice. Instead, I answered casually, "Marshall Lassiter. How about you?"

"Oh, I'll let a few of the guys bid on me." She added carelessly, "Marshall's a wonderful guy. He's intelligent and interesting to talk with."

That was just like Ramona. She was really rubbing it in. I guess she thought she had to remind me that only an "intelligent" boy would want to be my date. I couldn't possibly interest someone who was handsome or attractive. Marshall's intelligence was the only thing that could be admirable about him.

He had none of those things that made me so crazy about Jerod Crandall. And Ramona must have had Jerrod wrapped neatly around her little pinky. He had been her partner the previous year—and probably would be her partner again. Of course, I would be forced to eat with Marshall and endure a boring afternoon. The only thing I could say was that I probably wouldn't eat alone.

There were times when I think I hated Ramona. She was younger, had more curves, and had red highlights that made her hair stand out. My eyes and hair were plain; my voice was ordinary. I wasn't unattractive, but I wasn't a beauty like Ramona. I was drab in

166

contrast to her. And whenever I went out with her, the difference made me feel terribly uncomfortable.

It was the final blow when Ramona captured the one guy I really liked. And she just kept him trailing around with her menagerie of lovelorn men. While I had Marshall—and only Marshall. Then she had the nerve to tell me that she thought Marshall was wonderful.

I wasn't in a good mood the morning of the bake sale. We barely spoke to each other as we dressed. Dad thought it would be fun if we all rode together, so that's what we did. However, I didn't think any of it was fun.

I took our boxes over to the judge and took our numbers.

"Sixteen for me, Ramona, seventeen for Jeanette," she said laughingly, holding my slip out to me. "Remember that number, Marshall," she teased him then went gaily off to acquaint the herd with her number

Half an hour later the bidding began It was fun, but pretty cut and dried as far as competition went; since only one bid was made on three-quarters of the boxes. Then came number sixteen, Ramona.

Five guys started to bid on her box, and the bidding went on up to forty-eight dollars. There were only two guys left by then: Jerod Crandall and Pete Magnusson. Pete bid forty-nine, Jerrod topped him with fifty dollars, and got it.

The auctioneer bellowed: "Number sixteen goes to the gentleman in the gray sport shirt, and the lucky lady who will share her lunch with him is!" He looked down at his list and announced, "And the lady is Jeanette Eckert."

He drew my name out impressively, and a low murmur of surprise went through the crowd. But it was nothing compared to the surprise on Jerrod Crandall's face or my own amusement as I walked with hot cheeks and trembling legs to the platform.

By the time I'd received my box, the bidding had started on number seventeen. I heard Marshall bid twenty-five dollars. No competition was offered. The next thing I knew, Ramona's name was called and she went to get her box and partner.

What had happened was pretty obvious. Somehow our names and numbers had been mixed. What I could do was pretty obvious, too. I could just switch with Ramona.

That was the moment when my boldness appeared. Whether he liked it or not, I decided, I was not going to hand Jerod Crandall back to Ramona. I was going to have this lunch with him. Let Ramona lunch with Marshall and see what she thought of his intelligence at the end of two long hours.

So I hustled the bewildered Jerod back through the crowd. "I know a lovely spot way over in the grove where we can eat." I babbled, not adding what I was really thinking. I wanted a lovely secluded spot where Ramona wouldn't be able to find us.

Jerod was a good sport. If he felt cheated paying fifty dollars to have lunch with me instead of my beautiful sister, he didn't give any sign of it.

That lunch was a real treat! The same mood of daring that had prompted me to go off with Jerod carried me through it. It was do and die for me, so I acted wild and giddy for him. I laughed and sang and joked and mimicked our friends and the teachers we'd once had. I stuck leaves in my hair and danced in my bare feet.

For the first part of the lunch, Jerod sat like a man bemused. Then he laughingly joined me in my fun. We wound up going wading in the brook nearby. And once, when I slipped on a rock, he grabbed me to keep me from falling. But he didn't let me go.

"Jeanette," he said. "I never dreamed you were like this. All these years I've been chasing after Ramona, you were right under my nose and I didn't even see you." Then he kissed me, a sweet, long kiss.

I spent the rest of the day with Jerod. Later, we went to a restaurant, and then for a long drive. It was midnight before I got home. Because of the wonderful time I'd had, I felt like a princess in a fairy tale. But as I went up the walk I saw the light was on in our bedroom. Ramona was waiting up for me.

I prepared myself for her anger. Even if I got her to believe that I hadn't engineered the mix-up of our numbers, she'd still want to know why I had run away with Jerod instead of switching partners. I braced myself and walked into the bedroom.

Ramona came, white-faced, to meet me. "I can't even say I'm sorry, Jeanette," she told me steadily, "because I'm not. I couldn't help it. From the moment you brought him home, I knew he was for me. He's the only boy I know who doesn't think all a girl ever wants to hear is how gorgeous she is."

I was too stunned to answer. Ramona went on, "Jeanette, please don't hate me, but I love him so. It was so wonderful this afternoon talking to someone who knew what was going on in the world. Why, he—he didn't even try to kiss me. So you see, Jeanette," she finished quietly, "I just had to switch those numbers and ask Marshall to bid on me after Jerod got you."

I was shocked and thankful. Maybe I'll be forgiven for all the bitterness I stored up so unfairly against Ramona all those years. It doesn't matter, though. I stole my sister's boyfriend—and she's happy about it. Who would have thought that we each would get the man of our dreams.

THE END

168

A SPECIAL SISTER
I Can't Thank Her Enough

The relationship between sisters can be wide and varying. Some are close, the best of friends. Some have let sibling rivalry get in the way of any kind of closeness. Some have felt the hurt and pain received when rejected by a sister. Some, like me, have just felt distant.

With twelve years between us and my sister having left home for nursing school when I was still only a child of four, we had so little in common that there was no relationship at all other than being bound by blood. She was the oldest. I was the youngest. She was the brains of the family. I was the beauty. The only contact we really had, like everyone else in the family, was when someone was sick. Before we'd ever call a doctor, we would call Rosalie.

She didn't want me there. I knew that from the moment I made the phone call. I didn't want to be there. I knew that before I picked up the phone. This self-contained woman, whose only joy was found in her love of God and her endless reading, had very little use for the world outside her sheltered existence.

At seventy-five, she had lived her life and was patiently enjoying her solitude with the occasional exception of a neighbor or two dropping by to borrow a book or to check on her. No, I certainly wasn't wanted or needed—the little sister, the spoiled one, the one who had lived life to its fullest without much regard for siblings. I had always been apart, separated by age, by time and by sheer recklessness, traveling here and there without ever looking back.

When I was younger, I was sure that my pretty face and cute smile would get me whatever I wanted. Married three times and divorced three times, my reckoning had come. I was alone, broke, shunned by the very ones I held dear, emotionally distraught, and literally put out on the street with nothing but my clothes.

I picked up the phone to make the call that would change both of our lives. I remember asking her if I could stay for a few days until I figured out what to do and I still remember her very hesitant, "yes."

It was mid-November and chilly in the Midwest, a lot different than California, which had been my last stop. With my one suitcase in my hand mostly consisting of shorts and short-sleeved shirts, I rang the doorbell of her condo.

There she was, Rosalie, a heavy-set woman, ravaged by years and the illnesses that had robbed her of the ability to walk very far or even do any physical activity. Yet pity is the last word I would use to describe her: Strong, almost indestructible, with a keen intelligence that shone from her eyes. Cane in hand, she proceeded to welcome me not only into her condo, but also into her life.

Those first few days were the beginning of a slow and sometimes painful healing process that was to end up actually lasting a year and a half, during which I learned to laugh again and cry again, and to become strong maybe for the first time in both heart and mind. And, most of all, I learned to love my sister.

I think that the first thing I noticed about the condo is that my sister had no clue about decorating, or more than likely it didn't turn out quite as she had expected and she was too stubborn to admit it. From her lavender living room to her orange bedroom, it was a color scheme nightmare.

I asked her once why she didn't have it all painted a nice, pale green or an off-white and she retorted that she had seen enough of both colors at the hospital where she had been a nurse for many years before her retirement and she liked it just the way it was. So much for my input!

Though her condo consisted of two bedrooms, she had changed the extra one into an office. Although she did offer it to me, I could tell that she didn't want anything changed. So the hide-a-bed in the living room became mine. That was fine with me. Slowly the days became weeks and after a month or so, she did say that we should get a bed for me. By that time, though, I had become very comfortable where I was and didn't want to upset her routine. After all, I had no idea of how long I would be staying.

It was on one of those first few days that she decided that I needed to go shopping for a winter coat and some boots. I have to admit that I'm chicken when it comes to driving. I do have my license, but I hadn't driven in two years and certainly not anything like the tank of a car my sister had. Rosalie did drive that day, but she informed me that I would be driving soon.

Rosalie was a very religious person and spent as many mornings in church as her health would permit. I think it gave her the strength to go on despite all of her health problems. Though she was the mother of six, she didn't see her children often. Like my children, they had made their own lives and they were too busy raising their own to bother much with us.

I don't think they quite understood her, either. She could be very dominating and very opinionated, but if you dug deep enough she had a very generous heart. I am sure, too, that to them it seemed that she pushed them away.

It took me awhile before I understood that she quite honestly didn't know how to relate to her children. She loved them, I'm sure of that, but she showed her love by giving gifts of money instead of time. They never realized how much love went into her gifts. Sadly, her children also never realized how much she needed them to show they cared. A simple phone call once a week would've meant a lot to her, but it is a busy world out there and rarely did anyone take the time. And so we became closer, sharing companionship and eventually caring.

Shortly after Christmas, we both decided that I needed to look for a job. Again Rosalie hauled out the "tank," bundled up, and drove me around. Luckily I found one almost immediately at the local candy store. It was two blocks from her condo, within walking distance, though a bit breezy when the Chicago weather reached twenty below.

I enjoyed it there. It gave me a chance to get out and talk to people and it gave her a chance to enjoy that solitude she had missed when I ended up on her doorstep. Of course we both enjoyed the "sweet" benefits that I got a big discount on. She would be so happy when I'd bring a little box of her favorite candy home. And home it became. I think we both realized at the same time that I wouldn't be leaving any time soon.

By then she'd decided that it was time for me to start taking over the driving. The "tank" scared me. Because she had kept it in such perfect condition, I just knew that she would be devastated her if I got into an accident with it. I tried to explain that to her, but she would hear none of it.

Rosalie picked a cold and snowy day for me to have my first drive behind the wheel. I told her that she was mean, but she just laughed. I didn't understand at first that not only was she giving me driving lessons, she was also giving me my self-confidence back. Off we went, slipping and sliding, at a fantastic speed of about fifteen miles an hour first to church and then to the grocery store. We only got a few irate looks from other drivers. I was on a roll!

Many of our evenings were spent working on a puzzle, bickering good-naturedly over television programs, or just quietly reading together. We laughed. We argued. We became friends.

During the beginning months I was with her, she had a slight cough that never seemed to clear up. Concerned, I asked her if she'd had it checked. She answered that it had been going on since the previous August and she had an x-ray done. The results, though, were negative and she guessed that it was probably emphysema.

She wasn't too worried about it and began making plans for us to go to Mexico the following October, since she had a time-share there. She loved going there; mainly to sit by the pool, enjoy the scenery, and read. She had made it a habit to go twice a year and originally

171

had hoped her children would join her there in March, but though the plans had been made in advance, one by one they informed her they wouldn't be able to go. They had valid reasons—one couldn't take off from work, one had children in school, one had just started a new job, and one was having severe back pain—but they never knew how disappointed she was at that. It broke her heart, but again, she was a resilient woman and refused to be brought down by disappointment. Since I had just started a job I couldn't leave, so the big plan was for the fall. She and I would go together.

It was in February that she started mentioning that her side hurt. She was tired all the time and very short of breath. I think she was under the impression that her heart was acting up again. For Rosalie to even mention pain was very unusual. I encouraged her to get it checked, but stubborn as she was she wanted to wait for her next regular appointment, which she did.

Again an x-ray was taken and the doctor, unhappy with the results, ordered more tests. After receiving the results, the doctor referred her to a lung specialist. Rosalie, having been a nurse for many years and having already suffered through cancer twice, was pretty stoic about the whole thing. Either it was pneumonia or it was cancer.

I was the one who wasn't ready to accept it. Scared but trying to make light of it until we got definite results, we decided that if it weren't serious we would go on a shopping spree and redecorate her condo, and if it was serious we would, instead of crying about it, stop at the ice cream store and get a sundae.

Stage-four lung cancer hits you right between the eyes. The doctor was kind, but Rosalie insisted he not beat around the bush. She wanted the truth and he gave it to her. She was too far gone to have any cure, but he wanted her to see an oncologist to prolong her life as long as possible and to provide comfort when needed.

I looked at her in that doctor's office and wanted to cry. She gave me a look that said if I did she would be furious. I didn't cry, not then nor in the months that followed; at least not where she could see me. We left the office and went for that sundae. She insisted, though I don't think either of us tasted it.

The weekly trips to the oncologist started. At first she was against receiving chemotherapy, sure that there was no point since she was at already stage four. The oncologist was very persistent, though, and convinced her that the treatments would at least give her some time.

I remember sitting there when she asked him what kind of time she would get. If he could tell her that it would be quality time, then she would try it, but if it was just going to prolong the agony then she didn't want any part of it. He was honest when he told her he couldn't guarantee anything, but that he thought it would be quality time. He promised her that he would give her the lightest dose of chemo that he could and if she had an unbearable reaction to it he would stop it.

Two weeks later she received her first chemotherapy treatment. Sick does not describe her agony. This lasted for about four days and then she started to feel better. When she saw the oncologist again, she told him how she had felt and he thought she should try one more time. He thought that maybe because her hemoglobin was still low she had felt the effects more than she should have. She did try one more time and the effects were just as devastating, or possibly more so. She couldn't do it, she explained. She told the doctor no more chemotherapy.

Rosalie came home from that doctor's appointment and she was sure that she had only another month or so. God had different plans. I think He knew how much I still needed her. It was in June that she stopped the chemotherapy and I believe that was when she gave up. She cancelled the trip to Mexico that we were to take. She made immediate plans to get her affairs in order so that everything would be taken care of.

Her birthday was the following August. She was going to be seventy-six years old. I had wanted to have a big surprise party for her with all of her friends invited. Her children didn't think it would be a good idea and planned a nice dinner at a local restaurant instead. The dinner meant a lot to her, as everyone showed up. This was the first time in two years that her family was all together. Pictures were taken and she looked at them often in the following months.

I couldn't let go of the party idea, though, and got together with my niece, Chelsea, and planned that party. I am so glad I did. We worked together to make it a wonderful night. Chelsea invited Rosalie and me for dinner. Rosalie didn't want to go, but I laid it on real thick. I told her that we would really hurt Chelsea's feelings and that Rosalie had been promising to go over there for months. The clincher was when I told her that it might be the last time she could. So, she agreed, although she wasn't looking forward to it. She asked Chelsea if she would mind if we brought Rosalie's youngest daughter with us and, since we had planned on it anyway, Chelsea said of course.

Rosalie did insist on going to church that evening at five. Due to the ages of some of the guests, we'd planned the party for six o'clock. It would be cutting it close, but I was sure I could get us there.

It was only as we were leaving church, which had lasted longer than usual, I was told that instead of meeting her as planned, I had to pick up Rosalie's daughter who lived ten miles in the opposite direction and about fifteen miles from where we had to go. Since I had been designated driver ever since the chemotherapy, Rosalie expected my usual slow driving.

Not to be! I was in a hurry and so we flew. She couldn't believe it. I honestly think she was holding on to the side arm for dear life. She talked about that wild ride for months afterward, still shaking her head in disbelief.

We made it a little late, but not bad. As we pulled up Chelsea came to the driveway and asked Rosalie if she would come to the backyard to look at some plants she had back there. Totally unsuspecting, she did. I will always hold dear the look on her face, the wonder as she looked around at our brother who had driven in from a neighboring state with his family, old friends from her nursing days, friends from church, old neighbors, and her children, who had come together to pay homage to the woman who had given so much to all of us.

There were tears in her eyes, the only ones I had ever seen. They were tears of delight as she went from person to person expressing her joy at seeing them. It was a memorable evening for all of us, one that I will always hold close to my heart. It was an evening of happiness, watching as she opened her gifts. She laughed and she glowed. It was wonderful to see the sparkle in her eyes. Needles to say, the drive home was much more relaxed.

Rosalie held her own for the next several months. For a while it almost seemed the doctors were mistaken. Slowly, though, the pain became more intense. With her faith in God as strong as it was, she would wait for whatever He decided.

Christmas came and went and soon spring began to raise its fickle head, with one day bringing rain and the next sun. It was on a fateful day in March that I received the phone call that would haunt me for the rest of my life. It was from my daughter. She was coming to Chicago with my two young grandchildren and needed my help.

Torn between my sister and my daughter, I wasn't sure what to do. My grandsons, aged six and one, were the deciding factor. I had to leave. Rosalie made it clear that she couldn't handle them being there at the condo and I understood that. At the same time I couldn't leave them stranded. I called each of Rosalie's children and explained the problem and asked them to take over, checking on her daily. Gut-wrenchingly, I packed my things and left.

It was almost two months to the day after I left that Rosalie passed away. I was told that she was very serene. She had found her place in Heaven and could finally leave all of her suffering behind. To this day I can picture her, book in hand, resting on a cloud and directing everyone else up there.

Her funeral was simple, the way she had planned it. There was no eulogy and yet looking around I saw her eulogy in the faces of the people she had touched in her lifetime. There was the man in his eighties who'd brought her newspaper to her every day. He stood with tears in his eyes as he said his good-bye. There was the elderly woman who insisted on slipping me a twenty-dollar bill, wanting me to take my daughter to lunch in remembrance of my sister, who she swore saved her life when Rosalie was the nurse for the parish. There were the twin sisters who had asked her advice about their ill mother. There were so many people both young and old who had been touched by her throughout the years. All came with love, as did I.

If there were anything I could say to my sister now, it would simply be: "Thank you for laughter, for consolation, for hope, and, most of all, thank you for love."

THE END

Made in the USA
Middletown, DE
02 July 2017